Bus Alsina Greells.
Red white, green stripes

Andalucía

by Des Hannigan

Des Hannigan is a travel writer and
photographer who has written, and
contributed to numerous travel books and
guides, including *AA Essential Corfu,
AAA Travel Book Europe 2000* and
*AA Adventure Travellers India and
Himalayas.* When not travelling he lives in
the far west of Cornwall, England.

Above: *Plaza de Progreso; a typical Andalucían square
in Jerez de la Frontera*

Menue of the da
menu del día

AA Publishing

Above: Andalucía is always fascinating

Written by Des Hannigan
Updated by Mona King
Original Photography by Michelle Chaplow

Published by AA Publishing, a trading name of
Automobile Association Developments Limited,
whose registered office is Southwood East, Apollo
Rise, Farnborough, Hampshire, GU17 0JW
Registered number 1878835.

© The Automobile Association 2000, 2003, 2005

Reprinted May 2001. Reprinted 2003. Information
verified and updated.
This edition 2005. Information verified and updated.

Find out more about
AA Publishing and the
wide range of travel
publications and services
the AA provides by
visiting our website at
www.theAA.com/bookshop

A01990

Colour separation: Keenes, Andover
Printed and bound in Italy by Printer Trento S.r.l

Contents

About this Book

KEY TO SYMBOLS

✚ map reference to the maps found in the What to See section

✉ address or location

☎ telephone number

🕐 opening times

🍴 restaurant or café on premises or near by

🚇 nearest underground train station

🚌 nearest bus/tram route

🚆 nearest overground train station

🚢 ferry crossings and boat excursions

ℹ tourist information

♿ facilities for visitors with disabilities

✋ admission charge

↔ other places of interest near by

❓ other practical information

➤ indicates the page where you will find a fuller description

✈ travel by air

This book is divided into five sections to cover the most important aspects of your visit to Andalucía.

Viewing Andalucía pages 5–14
An introduction to Andalucía by the author.
Andalucía's Features
Essence of Andalucía
The Shaping of Andalucía
Peace and Quiet
Andalucía's Famous

Top Ten pages 15–26
The author's choice of the Top Ten places to see in Andalucía, each with practical information.

What to See pages 27–90
The four main areas of Andalucía, each with its own brief introduction and an alphabetical listing of the main attractions.
Practical information
Snippets of 'Did you know...' information
4 suggested drives
4 suggested walks
2 features

Where To... pages 91–116
Detailed listings of the best places to eat, stay, shop, take the children and be entertained.

Practical Matters pages 117–24
A highly visual section containing essential travel information.

Maps
All map references are to the individual maps found in the What to See section of this guide.
For example, Arcos de la Frontèra has the reference ✚ 28B2 – indicating the page on which the map is located and the grid square in which the town is to be found. A list of the maps that have been used in this travel guide can be found in the index.

Prices
Where appropriate, an indication of the cost of an establishment is given by € signs:
€€€ denotes higher prices, €€ denotes average prices, while € denotes lower charges.

Star Ratings
Most of the places described in this book have been given a separate rating:

🟦🟦🟦	Do not miss
🟦🟦	Highly recommended
🟦	Worth seeing

Viewing
Andalucía

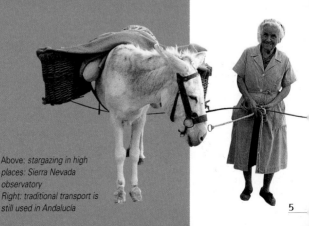

Above: *stargazing in high places: Sierra Nevada observatory*
Right: *traditional transport is still used in Andalucía*

5

Des Hannigan's Andalucía

Heritage is Progress
Andalucía has all the faults and foibles of any modern region. At times there is a heavy price to be paid, environmentally and aesthetically, for expansion and mass tourism. Improved communications mean that new roads slice across the landscape. Air quality in the traffic-logged streets of Granada and Seville can be very poor during the hottest months. Perhaps the best hope for this once bitterly poor region is that its astonishing beauty will survive the negative aspects of modern development as more and more people come to appreciate its heritage and landscapes.

Olive trees, a symbol of Andalucía

Andalucía is the reality that matches the dream. It is a land moulded by numerous influences, from those of prehistory to classical Rome, from medieval Arabia to 20th-century civil war. Of these, the Moorish influence has been the most enduring and seductive.

The landscapes of Andalucía are astonishingly varied. Beneath intensely blue skies lie vast fields of golden barley and yellow sunflowers, rolling hills of red and saffron-coloured earth studded with olive trees, dramatic desert 'badlands', the green foothills of the snow-capped Sierra Nevada and the rugged cliffs of countless lesser mountain ranges. Scattered across this vivid fabric lie the great cities, dramatic 'white towns' and clifftop villages that make Andalucía so alluring.

There is always an alternative here. You can enjoy the crowded high life of the Costa del Sol, find glamour and excitement in Seville and Granada or experience the flavour of North Africa in Almería province. You can stop the world in the shade of a village plaza, become immersed in the colourful festivals of remote villages, wander through cool labyrinths of Moorish streets or stumble across little-known baroque churches and elegant Renaissance buildings in sleepy provincial towns. And you can always find solitude among the distant mountains of the Sierra Cazorla, in the green foothills of Las Alpujarras, or along the lonelier stretches of the Atlantic coast.

Andalucía can be all things to all people, provided this intriguing and evocative land is explored with an open mind and with Andalucían enthusiasm.

Andalucía's Features

Geography
- Most southerly of Spain's 17 political regions or *Comunidades Autónomas* (Autonomous Communities).
- Eastern half of coastline borders the Mediterranean; western half borders the Atlantic.
- Area: 87,300sq km.
- Length of coastline: 800km.
- About one third over 600m high. Highest point: Mulhacén (3,482m), in the Sierra Nevada.
- Population: 7 million.

Climate
- Typical Mediterranean climate: hot, dry summers and mild, wet winters. Atlantic coast subject to the fierce wind known as the *Levante*, and to a hot dry wind called the *Sirocco* that blows from Africa.
- Average annual temperature: 17°C spring: 20°C; summer: 25°C; autumn: 18°C; winter: 13° C.
- Average annual rainfall: 500mm.
- Average hours sunshine each day: 9.

Agriculture
- Annual production of olives: 2 million tonnes; grain: 4 million tonnes; grapes: 6.5 million tonnes.
- Other products: oranges, lemons, bananas, melons, sugar cane, tomatoes, cucumbers, peppers, potatoes, cotton, tobacco, herbs, spices and flowers.
- *Plasticultura*, the intensive production of fruit and vegetables in huge plastic.greenhouses occupies large areas of the coastal plains east and west of Almería.
- Local specialities: cured ham (Sierra Morena and Las Alpujarras); horse-breeding (Jerez de la Frontera area); breeding of fighting bulls (hill country bordering Guadalquivir river valley).

Industry
- Mainly light industry, principally located along Guadalquivir Valley.
- Concentration of engineering, food-processing and textile-production at Seville.
- Tourism is a major contributor to the economy.

Roads
Andalucía's main roads were improved greatly during the late 20th-century. Today you can travel quickly and comfortably on dual carriageways between most main centres. Many rural roads have been improved, although you need to be prepared for a sudden deterioration in road surfaces, especially in mountain areas.

Inset: *fruitful Andalucía*
Below: *postcards from Córdoba*

7

Essence of Andalucía

Below: flamenco flair
Bottom: Bayarcal village at the heart of Las Alpujarras

Beyond the beaches of the Costa del Sol, and beyond the world-famous buildings of Seville, Granada and Córdoba, you will find the essence of Andalucía – in the towns and villages of the river plains, amidst the peaks and valleys of the Sierras and on the less developed Atlantic and Mediterranean coasts, such as the Costa de la Luz and the eastern section of the Costa de Almería. The vast size of Andalucía, the variety of its landscapes, the charm and individuality of its people will reward the visitor who is looking for the heart and soul of southern Spain.

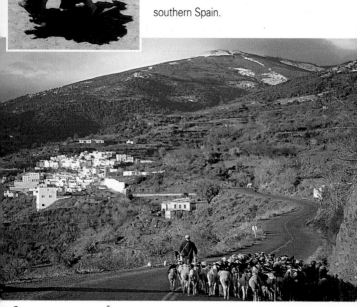

THE **10** ESSENTIALS

If you only have a short time to visit Andalucía, or would like to get a really complete picture of the country, here are the essentials:

• **Visit the world-famous attractions,** in spite of the crowds: Seville's cathedral and Giralda (➤ 81), Granada's Alhambra (➤ 16–17), Córdoba's Mezquita (➤ 21), make sure you take in the Alcazabas of Almería (➤ 52) and Málaga (➤ 63), as well.

• **Check to see whether there is a local festival** in the area you are visiting. If there is, make sure you attend. Be ready to party.

• **Seek out some of Andalucía's 'hidden gems'.** Visit the Casa de Pilatos mansion in Seville (➤ 80), the Cartuja in Granada (➤ 48), the Capilla del Salvador in Úbeda (➤ 25), the Iglesia de la Asunción in Priego de Córdoba (➤ 23).

• **Always take time** to relax at a café table while watching the world go by.

• **Visit the *pueblos blancos,*** the 'white towns' and hilltop villages of Málaga and Cádiz province, such as Zahara de la Sierra (➤ 26), Grazalema (➤ 71), Arcos de la Frontera (➤ 66), Vejer de la Frontera (➤ 75), and Medina Sidonia (➤ 71).

• **Go for a long walk** in Las Alpujarras (➤ 18), the Sierra Grazalema (➤ 71), the Sierra Morena (➤ 31) or the Sierra Cazorla (➤ 35).

• **See some flamenco** at a classical performance venue, at a festival, or at a *Peñas Flamencas,* a flamenco club. Ask at local tourist offices for details.

• **Eat Andalucían.** Try *gazpacho,* a delicious cold soup that comes in several forms, but always based on cucumber and tomatoes with olive oil and wine vinegar. Eat fish anywhere, but especially in Cádiz (➤ 67–8), or Sanlúcar de Barrameda (➤ 73). Above all, indulge yourself in *jamón serrano* or *pata negra,* the delicious cured ham of the Sierras; and sip *fino,* the driest and finest of sherries, as you go.

• **Try to visit at least two or three of the following:** Cádiz (➤ 67–8); Jerez de la Frontera(➤ 20); Priego de Córdoba (➤ 23); Baeza (➤ 36); Úbeda (➤ 25).

• **Browse in village shops** that are off the tourist trail. You will find some fascinating items that do not carry 'souvenir' prices.

Above left: *lunching at leisure on the seafront at Sanlúcar de Barrameda*
Above: a *colourful scene at Málaga during the annual fair*

The Shaping of Andalucía

25,000 BC
Cave paintings at Nerja and La Pileta indicate work of Late Palaeolithic hunter-gatherers.

4000–1500 BC
Neolithic settlement of Southern Spain from North Africa followed by Bronze Age introduction of metal-working. The important archaeological site of Los Millares dates from this period.

700–500 BC
Colonisation by Phoenicians, then by Greeks and finally by Carthaginians.

210 BC
Roman colonisation of Spain.

151 BC
Foundation of Córdoba as centre of Roman administration.

AD 409
Spain is invaded by Vandals. At this time, Southern Spain may have become known to North African Muslims as 'Vandalusia'.

711
Muslim forces capture Gibraltar and soon dominate 'al-Andalus'.

756
The Umayyad dynasty's emirate is established in Andalucía.

784
Work begins on mosque at Córdoba.

1031
End of centralised Muslim control as al-Andalus fragments into separate kingdoms.

1086
The Almoravids, a powerful Islamic sect, take control of al-Andalus.

1146
Almohads, independent Muslims with roots in Berber society, come to dominate al-Andalus.

Seville's La Giralda tower, an outstanding symbol of Islamic Spain

1163
Seville becomes the capital of al-Andalus. Building begins on the Giralda tower in 1184.

1236
The Christian King Fernando III captures Córdoba from the Moors.

1237
Granada becomes the centre of a shrinking Moorish Andalucía. The building of the Alhambra begins.

1248
Fernando III captures Seville from the Moors.

1469
The marriage of Fernando (Ferdinand) of Aragón and Isabel (Isabella) of Castile.

1487–9
Fernando and Isabel capture Málaga, Baeza and Almería.

1492
Unification of Spain completed when the last Moorish king of Granada, Boabdil, surrenders the city to Fernando and Isabel.

1568–70
Moriscos (Moors who had 'converted' to

Christianity) rebel against Christian rule. Las Alpujarras region becomes a Morisco area of refuge.

1609–11
The last remaining Moriscos are expelled from Spain.

1704
British capture Gibraltar.

1834
Andalucía is divided into eight provinces.

1924
King Alfonso XIII forced to share rule of Spain with dictator Miguel Primo de Rivera.

1931
Alfonso XIII goes into exile. Second Republic proclaimed.

1936–9
Civil War between incumbent Republicans and Nationalist rebels ends in victory for

Right: an upturned armoured car in Málaga during the Civil War

Nationalist forces under General Franciso Franco. The commencement of Franco's long dictatorship.

1968
Border with Gibraltar is closed by Spain.

1975
Death of Franco. Juan Carlos I, the grandson of Alfonso XIII, becomes king.

1982
The Sevillian politician, Felipe González becomes Prime Minister of Spain at head of first Socialist government since the Civil War. Andalucía becomes an Autonomous Community with its own Parliament in Seville and administered by a regional government: the Junta de Andalucía.

1985
Reopening of border between Spain and Gibraltar.

1986
Spain becomes a member of the European Community.

1992
World Exhibition (EXPO) held in Seville.

2002
The euro replaces the Spanish peseta as Spain's official currency.

Below: futuristic designs from Seville's Expo Fair in 1992

Peace & Quiet

Andalucía is such a large and varied country that opportunities for escaping the crowds are plentiful. Although the best places to find peace and quiet are in the hills and mountains of the interior, there are also large areas of undeveloped coastline to the east and west of the Costa del Sol.

Coastal Nature Parks & Reserves.

The coastal section of the distinctive Parque Natural de Cabo de Gata-Nijar is centred on the cape that makes up the eastern arm of Almería Bay. The waters off Cape Cabo de Gata have recently seen the reintroduction of the endangered Mediterranean monk seal. Las Salinas, the

area of salt pans just south of the village of Cabo de Gata, is noted for its thousands of migratory birds in spring and autumn.

Parque Nacional Coto de Doñana lies on the Atlantic seaboard to the west of Cádiz (➤ 67–8), and comprises the vast area of dunes and marshland of the delta of the River Guadalquivir. The Parque is one of Europe's largest and most important wetland areas, with over 250 bird species having been recorded.

Bird paradise in the Coto Doñana National Park

Inland Nature Parks & Reserves.

Parque Natural Sierra Maria is a large area of rugged limestone mountains near Vélez Blanco (➤ 59) in Almería province, with a rich cover of aleppo pines, larch and Scots pines. It harbours rare plants, eagles, and butterflies, and offers excellent walking opportunities.

Desierto de las Tabernas is famous for its use in the Clint Eastwood 'Spaghetti Western' films. The wider area is a semi-arid region of sculpted hills and gulches lying to the north of Almería (➤ 51–52). It has some unique plants and animals, and surprising oases of palm trees. It can be mercilessly hot.

The scenically spectacular Parque Natural Sierra de Grazalema is an area of mountains and wooded lesser hills surrounding the villages of Grazalema (➤ 71) and Zahara de la Sierra (➤ 26). One of the last refuges of the Spanish pine, the *pinsapo*, it is a superb walking and rock-climbing area, and is reputed to have the highest annual rainfall in Spain, so there's a possibility of cooling off.

Located inland from Tarifa (➤ 75), the Parque Natural de los Alcornocales harbours one of the world's largest areas of cork oak forest. There is a chance of spotting golden eagles, vultures, roe deer and red deer.

The Parque Natural Sierra Nevada, a huge area of high land south-east of Granada (► 44), contains the highest mountains in Andalucía, with Mulhacén its highest peak. The southern foothills of the area, Las Alpujarras (► 18), offer delightful walking opportunities through wooded valleys and terraces. The higher slopes are more rugged and dramatic.

The Parque Natural Sierras de Cazorla Segura y Las Villas is a marvellous area of mountains and forests, within which the River Guadalquivir has its modest source. Located in the northeast of Jaén province (► 39), this is the largest area of protected wilderness in Andalucía, with a great sense of remoteness off the beaten track. Griffon vultures, golden eagles, red deer and Spanish ibex are only a few of the more dramatic creatures to be seen here.

Inset: *walking in the Andalucian countryside*
Below: *in the beautiful Sierra Nevada*

Andalucía's Famous

Artists

Two of Spain's most famous painters, Diego Velázquez (1599–1660) and Bartolomé Esteban Murillo (1617–82) were born in Seville. Pablo Ruiz Picasso (1881–1973), one of the world's greatest artists, was born in Málaga. Picasso left Andalucía in his early teens to study in Barcelona and then in Madrid. He later moved to Paris. In Malaga, you can visit the Casa Natal Picasso (➤ 64), the birthplace of the artist, and the fine new Picasso Museum (➤ 65).

Musicians

Spain's most significant modern composer, Manuel de Falla (1876–1946) was born in Cádiz and lies buried in the city's cathedral crypt. Spanish folk music played a great part in de Falla's work. His most famous compositions are *Nights in the Garden of Spain* and the ballet *El Sombrero de Tres Picos* (*The Three-Cornered Hat*). Unhappy with Francoism, de Falla left Spain to live in Argentina, where he died.

The great Spanish guitarist, Andrés Segovia (1893–1987) was born in Linares in Jaén province. He was made Marquis of Salobreña by royal decree in 1981 and died in Madrid.

Right: *Manuel de Falla*
Below: *Andrés Segovia*

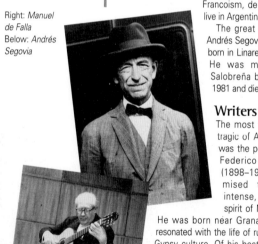

Writers

The most famous and most tragic of Andalucía's writers was the poet and playwright Federico García Lorca (1898–1936). Lorca epitomised the passionate, intense, yet life-affirming spirit of Moorish Andalucía. He was born near Granada and his work resonated with the life of rural Spain and with Gypsy culture. Of his best works, the most noted are the plays *Blood Wedding* and *The House of Bernarda Alba*, and the book of poems *Death of a Bullfighter*. Lorca was murdered by Francoite sympathisers. His body has never been found.

One of Andalucía's leading poets was Juan Ramón Jiménez (1881–1958), who was born in Moguer (➤ 90). His most famous work is *Platero and I*, a lyrical evocation of Moguer that he dedicated to his donkey, Platero.

Top Ten

Above: *ceramic ware from Úbeda*
Right: *intricate and colourful patterns are typical of Sevillan ceramics*

1
La Alhambra

✚ 44C2

✉ Calle Real, s/n

☎ 958 02 79 00

🕐 Mar–Oct, daily 8:30–8.
Floodlit visits Tue–Sat
10PM–11:30PM.
Nov–Feb, daily 8:30–6.
Floodlit visits Fri, Sat
8PM–9:30PM

🍴 Drinks and snack kiosk

🚌 Alhambrabus every 10
minutes: Plaza Isabel la
Católica–Plaza Nueva

♿ Few

✋ Expensive (free to
visitors with disabilities
and senior citizens; free
Sun after 3PM)

❓ Even out of season, you
are recommended to
pre-book your Alhambra
entry, as numbers are
restricted. Tickets can
be reserved up to one
year ahead by phoning
902 22 44 60 (in Spain)
or 0034 915 37 91 78
(from abroad). You can
also book via any branch
of Spain's BBV bank.
The main ticket gives
free-ranging access to
Alcazaba, Generalife
and Carlos V Palace; it is
marked with a half-hour
time slot permitting
entry to the Casa Real.

The International
Festival of Music and
Dance takes place at
various venues
throughout the
Alhambra from the end
of Jun to early July.

*La Alhambra is the greatest surviving expression
of Moorish culture in Spain, and is one of the
world's most spectacular heritage sites.*

La Alhambra (the Alhambra) stands on top of Granada's
Sabika Hill, against the background of the often snow-
covered massif of the Sierra Nevada. The 14th-century
Moorish poet Ibn Zamrak described Sabika as 'the garland
on Granada's brow', and the Alhambra as 'the ruby set
above that garland'. The walled complex is nearly 700m
long and about 200m wide. Its name is a corruption of the
Arabic *Al Qal'a al-Hamrá*, 'the red castle', a suggested
reference to the ruby-red sandstone walls of the Alcazaba,
the original fortress built on Sabika by the 11th-century
Emirs of Córdoba, and extended by later Islamic leaders.
The Alhambra's other Islamic buildings were established
during the 13th and 14th centuries by the Nasrites, the last
great Moorish rulers, at a time when most of Andalucía,
except for Granada and its less accessible hinterland, had
fallen to the 'Reconquest' of Catholic Spain.

There are four distinct groups of buildings within the
Alhambra: the Alcazaba, on the western escarpment of
Sabika; the Casa Real, the 14th-century Royal Palace of the
Sultans; the Palace of Carlos V, a late 15th-century
Renaissance addition; and the Palacio del Generalife, the
gardens and summer palace of the Sultans.

Right: *the lush gardens of
the Generalife, La
Alhambra*

Viewing the Alhambra in all its glory may take the best part of a day and there are usually crowds of fellow sight-seers. The heart of the Alhambra is the Casa Real, which reflects the ingenious manipulation of space and light and of cool water that was the special gift of Moorish architecture. The walls and roofs of its enthralling salons display exquisite stucco work, tiling and decorations that will take your breath away. Highlights include the stalactite vaulting of the Sala de los Abencerrajes and the intricately designed wooden ceiling of the domed Salón de Embajadores. The mood engendered amongst visitors is one of hushed awe.

Adjoining the Casa Real is the unfinished 16th-century Palacio de Carlos V, (Palace of Carlos V),an impressive example of High Renaissance architecture in spite of its rather uneasy intrusion on the essentially Moorish Alhambra. The palace's circular courtyard, segmented by sharply defined *sol y sombra*, 'sunlight and shade', was once used as a bull ring. To the west of the palace is the fortified Alcazaba, a distinctively older, more rugged monument than the sophisticated domestic buildings of the Casa Real. From the Alcazaba's Vela tower there is a spectacular view of Granada spread out below and of the high ground of the Sierra Nevada massed across the southern skyline. At the eastern end of the Alhambra complex, on *Cerro del Sol*, the Hill of the Sun, lies the luxurious Generalife, a captivating world of tinkling fountains and mirrored pools.

You can reach the Alhambra on the special *Alhambrabus* (see panel), by taxi, or by car, following prominent signs along the city's ring-road to a car park near the ticket office. Or you can walk from the Plaza Nueva by following the steep and narrow street, Cuesta de Gomérez, to the Alhambra's monumental Renaissance entrance gateway, the Puerta de las Granadas ('Gate of the Pomegranates'). The entrance is farther uphill.

Main picture: *La Alhambra viewed from the Albaíci*
Inset: *the Patio de los Leones, the Court of the Lions at the heart of La Alahambra's Casa Real (Royal Palace)*

2
Las Alpujarras

29E2

Southern Sierra Nevada, Granada province

Bars and restaurants in most villages €–€€

Granada–Alpujarra
☎ 958 18 54 80

Fiesta de San Antonio, Trevélez, 13–14 Jun. Pilgrimage to the peak of Mulhacén from Trevélez, 5 Aug

A typical village in Las Alpujarras

The southern foothills of the Sierra Nevada, known as Las Alpujarras, were the last stronghold of Moorish influence in medieval Spain.

The hills of Las Alpujarras descend in green waves to the arid river valleys of the Río Guadalfeo in the west and the Río Andarax in the east. On the south side of these valleys lie the Sierra de Contraviesa and the Sierra de Gádor, mountain barriers that shut out the populous and developed Almerían coast. A more ancient people than the Moors first carved out cultivation terraces and irrigation channels on the hillsides, but the region's history as the final enclave of the *Moriscos*, nominally Christianised Moors, has given Las Alpujarras much of its romantic appeal.

This is complex and enchanting countryside, which offers superb walking. Driving in Las Alpujarras can also be a pleasure, provided you accept that it may take you all day to drive 50km along the great shelf of hills. Narrow, serpentine roads bend to the terraced slopes and sink discreetly into the valleys. Ancient villages and hamlets such as Bayárcal, Yegen and Bérchules invite relaxing halts. The flat-roofed, North African-style houses of the villages are painted white now, but originally the bare stone walls merged with the landscape.

At the heads of the deepest western valleys in the 'High Alpujarras' lie popular villages such as Trevélez, 'capital' of *jamón serrano*, the famous cured ham of the mountains. Further west is the Poqueira Gorge, a deep valley striking into the heart of the Sierra Nevada. Clinging to its slopes are the charming villages of Pampaneira, Bubión and Capileira, from where the wild country of the Sierra is easily reached on foot. (▶ 54).

3
Gruta de las Maravillas, Aracena

The spectacular limestone formations of Aracena's underground cave system, the Gruta de las Maravillas, are the finest in Andalucía.

➕ 28B3

✉ Pozo de la Nieve s/n

☎ 959 12 82 06/959 12 83 55

🕐 Daily 10:30–1:30 and 3–6. Mon–Fri tours every hour. Sat–Sun tours every half-hour

🍴 Restaurante Casas

🚌 Daily Huelva-Aracena, daily Seville-Aracena

♿ None

✋ Moderate

❓ Tickets booked at the tourist centre opposite caves entrance. At busy periods your entry time may be an hour or two ahead

Spectacular limestone formations inside the Gruta de las Maravillas

Aracena's limestone caves, the Gruta de las Maravillas (Grotto of Marvels, or Cavern of the Wonders) comprise nearly 1.2km of illuminated galleries and tunnels that are open to the public. These galleries link 12 spectacular caverns, where limestone deposits have formed stalactites and stalagmites and densely layered flows of calcium carbonate known as tufa. There are six small lakes within the system and the whole is linked by paved walkways, ramps and steps. Carefully arranged lighting adds to the effect and piped music, specially written for the site, murmurs in the background. (Note that the caves can be quite chilly.)

Guided tours of the caves are accompanied by commentary in Spanish, but non-Spanish speakers will still enjoy a visually stunning experience. Stay near the back of the crowd and you will have time to admire the fantastic natural architecture that often seems to mirror, with grotesque exaggeration, the intricate decoration of baroque altars and Mudéjar façades of Andalucían churches. The caverns all have special names, and the guide points out lifelike figures and faces on the convoluted walls and roofs. The final cavern, known famously as the *Sala de los Culos*, the 'Room of the Backsides', is exactly that: a hilarious extravaganza of comic rude bits, of huge limestone phalluses and entire tapestries of pink tufa buttocks. You will hear groups of elderly Spanish ladies at the head of the throng shriek with laughter as they reach this part of the tour.

4
Jerez de la Frontera

28B2

35km (22m) north east of Cádiz, 83km (52m) south of Seville

Numerous restaurants and bars (€–€€€)

Estacíon de Ferrocarril, Plaza de la Estacíon s/n
☎ 956 34 23 19

Estacíon de Autobuses, c/ Cartuja
☎ 956 34 52 07

Few

Alameda Cristina
☎ 956 33 11 50;
www.webjerez.com

Semana Santa (Holy Week). Horse Fair, early May. Vendemia, wine festival, early Sep

Moorish style at Jerez de la Frontera's 11th-century Alcázar

Jerez de la Frontera has given its name to sherry, one of the most popular drinks in the world. It is also a centre of equestrianism and flamenco.

The rich chalky soil of the Jerez area supported vine-growing from the earliest times. Today the coastal region that lies south of a line between Jerez and Sanlúcar de Barrameda (➤ 73) is the official sherry-producing area, the Marco de Jerez. The famous sherry-producing bodegas of Jerez are where fermented wine, produced mainly from white Palomino grapes, is stored and transformed into sherry, and where brandy is also produced. Tours of bodegas end with a pleasant tasting session, confirming the precise distinctions between dry *Fino* and the darker and sweeter *Oloroso* and *Amontillado*.

Jerez's other famous institution is the Real Escuela Andaluza del Arte Ecuestre (Royal Andalusian School of Equestrian Art) at Avda Duque de Abrantes: the horse riding displays should not be missed. Jerez has excellent cafés, restaurants and shopping, especially in its pedestri-anised main street Calle Larga. Rewarding visits can be made to the restored 11th-century Alcázar and Arab Baths, the delightful Plaza de la Asunción and the Barrio Santiago, Jerez's old gypsy or *gitano* quarter, with its narrow lanes and old churches. In the Barrio you can visit the Museo Arqueológico (Archaeological Museum) in Plaza del Mercado and see archive material and audio visual presen-tations about Flamenco, at the Centro Andaluz de Flamenco in the Plaza de San Juan.

5
La Mezquita (Córdoba)

*Of all the Moorish buildings to survive in
Andalucía, the Great Mosque of Córdoba is the
most haunting and the most Islamic in its forms.*

➕ 32B2

✉ c/ Torrijos 10

☎ 957 47 05 12

🕐 Mon–Sat 10–7, Sun 2–7

🍴 Restaurante Bandolero,
c/ de Torrijos 6 (€€)

🚉 Estación de Ferrocarril,
Avenida de América

♿ Few

✋ Moderate

*The magnificent columns
and the arches of
Córdoba's Mezquita*

The Mezquita (Mosque) of Córdoba was begun in 785 and
expanded and embellished during the following two
centuries. You enter the complex by the Patio de los
Naranjos, the Courtyard of the Orange Trees, where
numerous fountains once sparkled in the dappled shade
and where Moslem worshippers carried out ritual
ablutions. The mosque itself is then entered through the
modest Puerta de Las Palmas. Immediately, you are
amidst the thickets of columns and arches that are the
enduring symbol of the Mezquita. Smooth pillars of
marble, jasper and onyx, plundered from the building's
Roman and Visigothic predecessors, supplement the total
of over 1,200 columns supporting the horseshoe arches of
red brick and white stone. At the far end of the vast
interior you will find the *Mirhab*, the prayer niche of the
mosque, a breathtaking expression of Islamic art.

At the very centre of the Mezquita stands the 1523
Renaissance cathedral of Carlos V, an intrusion that
reflected Christian pride rather than piety. Carlos later
admitted that the addition of the cathedral had 'destroyed
something that was unique in the world'. The cathedral's
presence is cloaked by the surrounding pillars of the
mosque and made somehow less obvious, although it is
the focus of worship today. Its carved mahogany choir
stalls are outstanding and there are other striking baroque
features, but it is the Islamic Mezquita, with its forest of
columns and swirling arches, that is most compelling.

6
Parque Natural el Torcal

🕂 29D2

✉ Centro de Recepcíon,
Parque Natural el Torcal,
Antequera

☎ 95 20 313 89

🕐 Reception Centre; daily
10–5

🍴 Café (€€)

♿ Few

↔ Antequera (➤ 66)

On the road to El Torcal

El Torcal and its spectacular rock formations lies 13km south of the town of Antequera and is one of the most remarkable of Andalucía's Natural Parks.

The limestone pinnacles and cliffs of the Sierra del Torcal cover an area of 1,171ha. The name *Torcal* derives from the word for 'twist' and aptly sums up the maze of narrow vegetation-filled gullies and ravines among the towering reefs and pillars of rock. From the visitors' car park there are several waymarked circular walking routes through the labyrinth. The shortest route tends to be crowded but there are longer circular routes, and well-worn paths into the labyrinth can be followed, and then retraced. An early morning or late afternoon visit is recommended.

The dense undergrowth is formed from holm oak, hawthorn, maple and elder; ivy clings to the rock faces. Countless flowering plants include saxifrage, peony, rock buttercup, rock rose, thistle and numerous species of orchid. El Torcal's general isolation supports a rich bird life that includes the great grey shrike, vultures and eagles, as well as numerous small perching birds. There is a good chance of spotting the harmless but fierce-looking ocellated lizard, the largest lizard in Europe.

A reception centre at the entrance to El Torcal has an exhibition and audio-visual display with excellent information about the geology and wildlife of the area. Exhibits are labelled in Spanish only. A short path leads from near the reception centre to the Mirador de las Ventanillas, a spectacular viewpoint.

7
Priego de Córdoba

The charming Córdoban town of Priego de Córdoba is rich in Baroque architecture and offers a rare insight into provincial Andalucía.

From Priego's central square, the handsome Plaza de la Constitución, the broad Calle del Río leads southeast past the churches of Our Lady of Anguish and Our Lady of Carmen to a peaceful square containing two splendid fountains. These are the 16th-century Fuente del Rey, with its handsome sculpture of Neptune and Amphitrite, and the more restrained Renaissance fountain, the Fuente de la Virgen de la Salud.

From busy Plaza Andalucía, adjoining the Plaza de la Constitución, walk north-east down Solana and through the Plaza San Pedro to a junction with Calle Doctor Pedrajas. To the left is a 16th-century slaughterhouse, the Carnicerías Reales, beautifully preserved with an arcaded patio, from where a superb stone staircase descends to a basement. Turning right along Calle Doctor Pedrajas brings you to the Plaza Abad Palomina and the privately owned Moorish Castillo. Priego's greatest baroque monument, the Iglesia de la Asunción (Church of the Ascencion), is at the far corner of the square. Its plain, whitewashed exterior gives no indication of the treasures inside, a beautifully carved *retablo* (altarpiece) and a spectacular *sagrario* (sacristy), an extravaganza of white stucco, frothing with emblems and statues beneath a cupola pierced by windows.

From delightful little Plaza de Santa Anna, alongside the church, head into the Barrio de la Villa down Calle Real, and wander through the maze of this old Moorish quarter, now bedecked with flowers. Stroll along Calle Jazmines to find the Paseo de Adarve, an airy Moorish promenade with superb views to the surrounding hills, an elegant final flourish to Priego's charms.

➕ 29D3

✉ 65km southeast of Córdoba, 60km northwest of Granada

🍴 Numerous restaurants and bars (€–€€€)

🚌 Granada–Priego, Córdoba–Priego. Estación de Autobuses, c/ San Marcos

ℹ c/ Río 33 Mon–Sat 10–1
☎ 957 70 06 25

♿ Few

↔ Zuheros (➤ 41); Montefrío (➤ 55)

The Fuente del Rey, "The King's Fountain" is in the centrepiece of this square in Priego de Córdoba

8
Reales Alcázares (Seville)

78B3

Plaza del Triunfo

954 50 23 23

Tue–Sat 9:30–7, Sun 9:30–5

Numerous cafés and restaurants in surrounding streets (€–€€€)

C1, C2, C3, C4

Avda de la Constitución 21B ☎ 954 22 14 04/954 21 81 57; www. turismo.sevilla.org

Few

Moderate; children under 12 and senior citizens free

Cathedral and Giralda (►81)

A visit early or late in the day may win you some added space. At busier times, numbers are regulated and you may have to wait your turn

The Royal Palaces of Seville are a fine example of Mudéjar building – Moorish-influenced post-Conquest architecture.

After Sevilla (Seville) fell to Christian forces in 1248, the Spanish king Pedro the Cruel reshaped and rebuilt much of the city's original Alcázar in Mudéjar style. It is this version that survives at the heart of the present complex, in spite of many restorations and in spite of the often clumsy additions made by later monarchs.

Highlights of the Alcázar include the Chapel of the Navigators, where Isabella of Castile masterminded the conquest of the Spanish Americas. The room's coffered wooden ceiling, a classic example of *artesonado* style, is studded with golden stars. Inside the palace proper is the Patio of the Maidens, with fine stucco work and *azulejos* tiling. Beyond lies the Salón de Carlos V, with another superb *artesonado* ceiling and then the Alcázar's finest room, the Salon of the Ambassadors, crowned by a glorious dome of wood in green, red and gold and with a Moorish arcade.

Adjoining the main palace are the dull and cavernous chambers of the Palacio de Carlos V, added by that insatiable intruder upon fine buildings, the Hapsburg king. These lead to the serene and lovely gardens of the Alcázar, where an arc of water from a high faucet crashes spectacularly into a pool in which a bronze statue of Mercury stands in front of a rusticated façade: the Gallery of the Grotesque. The rest of the gardens are a pleasant conclusion before you emerge into the Patio de las Banderas with Seville's mighty cathedral beckoning ahead.

Right: *Mudejar arches in the Reales Alcázares*
Below: *fresco of Neptune*

9
Úbeda

Although famous for its Moorish architecture Andalucía also boasts some of Spain's finest Renaissance buildings. Úbeda has some of the best.

✠ 29E3

✉ 45km northeast of Jaén

🍴 Numerous restaurants and bars (€–€€€)

🚌 Daily, Jaén–Úbeda, Granada–Úbeda, Baeza–Úbeda

ℹ Palacio del Marqués del Contadero, c/ Baja del Marqués 4
☎ 953 75 08 97

♿ Few

❓ Fiesta de San Miguel, 4 Oct

The façade of the Sacra Capilla del Salvador in the peaceful Plaza de Vázquez de Molina

Renaissance Úbeda survives triumphantly within its more modern and often featureless surroundings. To reach the crowning glory of the Plaza de Vázquez de Molina, you need to navigate the urban maze from the town's modern centre at the busy Plaza de Andalucía. From here the narrow, Calle Real runs gently downhill to the Plaza del Ayuntamiento, where a short street leads to the glorious enclave of Plaza de Vázquez de Molina. Just before entering the Plaza, you will find, on the right, Úbeda's remarkable Museo de Alfarería (Pottery Museum), which is well worth a visit.

On the right as you enter Plaza de Vázquez de Molina is the Palacio de las Cadenas, the work of the great classical architect Andrés Vandelvira. Directly opposite is the handsome Church of Santa María de los Reales Alcázares, enclosing a lovely Gothic cloister on the site of an original Moorish building. East of here lie other fine buildings, culminating in a 16th-century palace, now Úbeda's luxurious Parador hotel (► 100).

At the east end of the Plaza is the Sacra Capilla del Salvador. This private burial chapel dates from the mid-16th century and was completed by Vandelvira to an earlier design. The grand exterior apart, inside you will find a carefully restored *retablo* (altarpiece) of breathtaking splendour, beneath a soaring cupola. Other fine buildings and churches are found in Plaza San Pedro, reached from halfway down Calle Real, and in Plaza del Primero de Mayo, just north of Plaza de Vázquez de Molina.

10
Zahara de la Sierra

Hailed as one of the finest of the pueblos blancos, ('white towns') of Ronda, Zahara de la Sierra occupies a spectacular hilltop position.

✝ 28C2

✉ 22km northwest of Ronda

🍴 Restaurants and bars (€–€€)

🚌 Daily, Ronda–Zahara de la Sierra

ℹ c/San Juan
☎ 956 12 31 14

♿ Few

↔ Grazalema (▶ 71)

❓ Corpus Christi, end May–early Jun

The gleaming white buildings of Zahara against the backdrop of the Moorish castle

The red-roofed, white-walled houses of the lovely village of Zahara cluster beneath a dramatic hilltop castle at the heart of the Sierra Margarita in the Parque Natural Sierra de Grazalema. Below, to the northeast, is a large reservoir, the Embalse de Zahara formed by damming the Río Guadalete. Zahara's castle has Roman origins but was rebuilt by the Moors during the 12th century. It was later occupied by Christians, and its reckless retaking by the forces of Granada's Nasrid rulers in 1481 prompted Ferdinand and Isabella to launch the final conquest of Moorish Granada and its province.

If you visit Zahara by car, it is best to find a roadside parking space near the top of the steep approach road before entering the centre of the village. Zahara is a delightful hilltop enclave, its Moorish character intact. The castle has been recently renovated and is reached from the village square by following a winding pathway uphill past a charming cave fountain. The views from the castle and its tower are spectacular, but take care on the steep, unlit steps. The tiny village square stands in front of the baroque church of Santa María de la Mesa and there is an airy *mirador*, a viewing balcony, overlooking the reservoir. At the other end of the main street, at the entrance to the village, is the little church of San Juan, which harbours some vivid statues. At night Zahara's castle is floodlit and its centre and side streets take on a charming intimacy.

What To See

Above: *a relaxed way of
sightseeing in Córdoba*
Right: *modern tourists
beneath the ancient walls of
Córdoba's Alcázar*

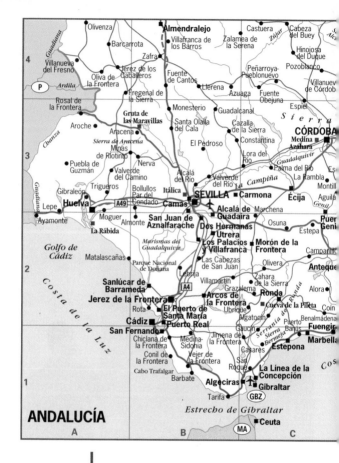

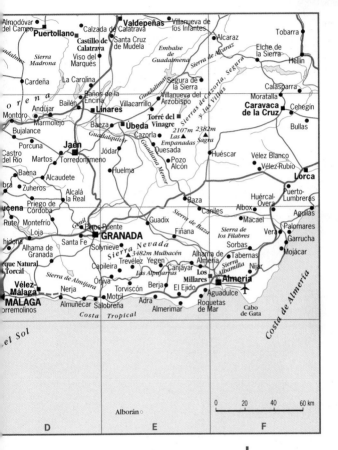

Córdoba and Jaén

The provinces of Córdoba and Jaén are where Moorish and Renaissance Spain overlap and where a more northern European influence has imposed itself on Mediterranean Andalucía. The Río (river) Guadalquivir neatly divides Córdoba province, and the city of Córdoba stands on its northern banks. To the north and west lie the smooth, wooded hills of the Sierra Morena; south is the farming country of the Campiña, dotted with olives and vines and patched with fields of golden grain. Here lie delightful towns and villages such as Priego de Córdoba and Zuheros.

The city of Jaén, and its nearby towns of Baeza and Úbeda – all more Renaissance than Moorish – sit at the centre of Jaén province, a landscape of regimented olive trees, where low hills extend towards the dramatic mountain wall of the Sierra Cazorla in the east.

> *'Oh fertile plain, oh soaring hills. Favoured by the sky and gilded by the day'*
>
> LUIS DE GÓNGORA, 1627

●

Above: *the Mezquita, Córdoba's famous mosque*
Left: *Moorish skills at harnessing water helped create beautiful gardens such as those of Córdoba's famous mosque*

Córdoba

Modern Córdoba is a small city with a big heart. It has an engaging intimacy not found in Granada or Seville and is less traffic-bound than these main urban centres. The pedestrianised central areas of modern Córdoba merge satisfyingly with the narrow streets of the Judería, the old quarter that encloses the Mezquita, Córdoba's world-renowned

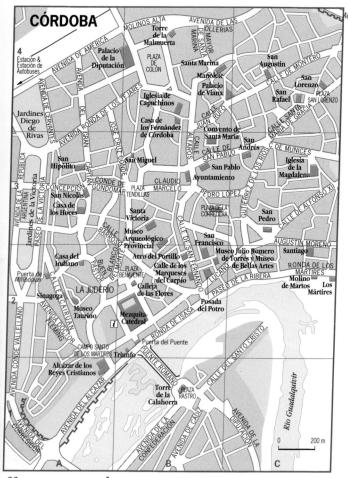

CÓRDOBA

4
Estación &
Estación de
Autobuses

AVENIDA DE AMÉRICA

MOLINOS ALTA

Torre de la Malmuerta

AVENIDA DE LAS OLLERIAS

MAYOR DE SANTA MARINA

Palacio de la Diputación

PLAZA DE COLÓN

Santa Marina

San Augustin

CALLE DE MONTERO

San Lorenzo

PLAZA SAN LORENZO

Manolete

Palacio de Viana

San Rafael

AVENIDA DE CERVANTES

RONDA DE LOS TEJARES

Iglesia de Capuchinos

CALLE JUAN RUFO

Jardines Diego de Rivas

DEL GRAN CAPITÁN

JOSÉ CRUZ CONDE

Casa de los Fernández de Córdoba

CALLE ALFAROS

Convento de Santa María

San Andrés

CALLE SANTA MARÍA DE GRACIA

San Hipólito

San Miguel

CALLE DE SAN PABLO

San Pablo

DE MUNICES

Iglesia de la Magdalena

AVENIDA DE LA REPÚBLICA

San Nicolás

CONCEPCIÓN

CONDE DE GONDOMAR

PLAZA TENDILLAS

CLAUDIO MARCELO

Ayuntamiento

PEDRO LOPEZ

GUTIÉRREZ DE LOS RIOS

CALLE DE ALFONSO XI

AVENIDA DE LA ARGENTINA

Casa de los Hoces

Jardines de la Victoria

PASEO DE LA VICTORIA

CALLE BARROSO

BUEN PASTOR

Santa Victoria

PLAZA DE LA CORREDERA

San Pedro

Puerta de Almodóvar

AVENIDA CONDE VALLELLANO

Casa del Indiano

CALLE CAIRUÁN

AVENIDA DOCTOR FLEMING

BLANCO BELMONTE

Museo Arqueológico Provincial

Arco del Portillo

PLAZA BENAVENTE

CALLE DE SAN FERNANDO

San Francisco

Calle de los Marqueses del Carpio

LUCANO

Museo Julio Romero de Torres y Museo de Bellas Artes

PASEO DE LA RIBERA

AUGUSTÍN MORENO

Santiago

RONDA DE LOS MÁRTIRES

Molino de Martos

Los Mártires

Sinagoga

LA JUDERÍA

Museo Taurino

Calleja de las Flores

Mezquita-Catedral

Posada del Potro

Puerta del Puente

RONDA DE ISASA

CAMPO SANTO DE LOS MÁRTIRES

Triunfo

PUENTE ROMANO

CALLE DEL SANTO CRISTO

Río Guadalquivir

AVENIDA DEL ALCÁZAR

Alcázar de los Reyes Cristianos

Torre de la Calahorra

PLAZA RASTRO

AVENIDA DE LA CONFEDERACIÓN

AVENIDA DE CADÍ

AVENIDA DE LA DIPUTACIÓN

AVENIDA DEL CORREGIDOR

0   200 m

A   B   C

mosque, a breathtaking survivor of Moorish Andalucía. In hidden corners of the city, away from the more crowded areas you will feel the engaging spirit of an older Spain.

Córdoba has a spectacular past. In 152BC the Romans founded their settlement of *Corduba* on the banks of the Río Guadalquivir, and for six centuries the city flourished, enriched by trade in olive oil, minerals and wool. Moorish conquest in the 8th century eventually made Córdoba a glittering rival to Baghdad as a centre of Islamic culture. A visit to the ruins of the 10th-century palace of **Medina Azahara** (open Tue–Sat and Sun mornings), a few kilometres outside the city, gives some perspective on Córdoba's importance during the Moorish period. In the 11th century the heavy hand of the Christian Reconquest signalled the beginning of the city's decline, until 20th-century agriculture, light industry and tourism shaped the flourishing Córdoba of today.

You can enjoy life here without feeling overpowered by too many competing attractions. Yet Córdoba has all the modern facilities of a major centre. It also has great style, reflected in its mix of lively bars and cafés and top quality restaurants, and in its fashionable shops and clothes-conscious young people. The happy merging of the past with the present is what makes Córdoba so appealing.

🛈 Calle Torrijos 10
✉ 957 47 12 35; fax 957 49 17 78

Medina Azahara
✠ 28C3
✉ 7km west of Córdoba, on the CP199 off the A431
☎ 957 32 91 30
♿ Few
💰 Cheap (Free to EU passport holders)

Main picture: *view from the Roman Bridge of the Puerta del Puente, the 'Gate of the Bridge'*
Inset: *coach driver outside the Mezquita*

The gardens of Córdoba's Alcazar display the lushness and coolness of Moorish Andalucía

What to See in Córdoba

ALCÁZAR DE LOS REYES CRISTIANOS

Córdoba's Alcázar de los Reyes Cristianos (Palace of the Christian Kings) is an interesting hybrid of Christian and Moorish features that epitomise the Mudéjar architectural styles of medieval Andalucía. It was built during the late 13th century, soon after the Reconquest, as a palace for the Christian monarchs. The building houses a museum in which there are some outstanding Roman mosaics. The gardens are real sun traps and blaze with colourful flowerbeds and shrubs, while ponds and fountains glitter in the unforgiving sunlight. Cool interiors compensate for the heat.

JUDERÍA

The engaging maze of narrow alleys that lies between the Plaza Tendillas and the Mezquita is the Judería, Córdoba's old Jewish quarter. The area of the Judería close to the Mezquita is given over to souvenir shops, but there is still much charm in popular venues such as the flower-bedecked Callejón de las Flores, a narrow cul-de-sac whose walls neatly frame the Mezquita's old minaret tower. At c/Maimónides 18, near the Museum of Bullfighting, there is a 14th-century synagogue, the only one in Andalucía and a good example of Mudéjar architecture. Near the synagogue is the Puerta de Almodóvar, a 14th-century city gate flanked by a statue of the Roman scholar, Seneca, who was born in here.

LA MEZQUITA (▶ 21, TOP TEN)

MUSEO ARQUEOLÓGICO PROVINCIAL

Córdoba's Museo Arqueológico Provincial (Archaeological Museum) occupies a delightful Renaissance mansion, the Palacio de los Páez. The arcaded entrance patio (a well-known Córdoban feature), along with the building's overall charm, its coffered ceilings and elegant staircases, enhances the excellent displays of prehistoric, Roman and Moorish exhibits. These include Roman mosaics and tombstones, and a subtle Moorish bronze in the form of a stag, found at the ruins of Medina Azahara (▶ 33).

32A1
Plaza Campo Santo de los Mártires
957 42 01 51
Tue–Sat 10–2, 4:30–6:30, Sun 9:30–2:30
Bar-Restarante Millán, Avda Dr Fleming 14 (€€)
Few
Moderate; free Tue
The Mezquita (▶ 21)

32B3
Numerous bars, cafés and restaurants (€€–€€€)

32B3
Plaza Jerónimo Páez
957 47 04 11
Tue 2:30–8:30, Wed–Sat 9–8:30, Sun 9–2:30
Several cafés (€–€€€)
Few
Cheap/free

A Drive Through the Sierras

This is quite a long drive with a great deal to see. An overnight stop at somewhere like Segura de la Sierra is worthwhile.

From Úbeda go east along the N322, signed Valencia, Albacete. After 2km, bear right, signed Cazorla. Watch carefully for a Halt sign and at a roundabout, take the exit signed A315, Cazorla.

The road winds pleasantly towards distant mountains through low hills covered with olive trees. Fields of wheat and barley shine like gold in early summer.

At the main square of Cazorla (➤ 37) go round the roundabout then bear right along the road marked 'Sierra' on its surface. Pass La Iruela village, where a ruined castle stands on a rock pinnacle. At Burenchal take the right fork, signed Parque Natural. Follow the winding A319 through magnificent scenery. After 15km, go left at a junction signed Coto Ríos.

The road follows the Guadalquivir valley through beautiful wooded mountains, passes the visitors' centre at Torre del Vinagre, then runs alongside the Tranco reservoir.

Two thirds of the way along the reservoir, cross a dam and keep right at the junction. After 9km, at a junction below the hilltop village of Hornos, go left, signed Cortijos Nuevos. Go through Cortijos and at roundabout take second right, signed La Puerta de Segura. Continue on the A317 and follow signs for La Puerta de Segura and Albacete. Drive carefully through Puerta de Segura, then follow signs for Puente de Genave and Úbeda. Join the N322 and return to Úbeda.

Distance
214km

Time
8 hours

Start/End point
Úbeda
✚ 29E3

Lunch
La Montería (€€)
✉ Plaza de la Corredera 18, Cazorla
☎ 953 72 12 01

Hornos village, perched on its rocky bluff at the heart of the Sierras

35

What to See in Córdoba and Jaén

BAEZA ✪✪✪

🏛 29E3

✉ 48km northeast of Jaén

🍴 Numerous restaurants and bars (€–€€€)

🚌 Daily, Jaén-Baeza, Granada–Baeza, Úbeda–Baeza

🚉 Railway station at Linares-Baeza, 14km from Baeza; connecting buses.

ℹ Plaza del Pópulo s/n
☎ 953 74 04 44

♿ Few

❓ Semana Santa, Mar/Apr. Romería del Cristo de la Yedra, 7 Sep

Above: *Baeza's Catedral de Santa María towers over the lovely Plaza de Santa María and it's 16th-century fountain*
Right: *Cazorla, dominated by the old Moorish castle, La Yerda, with, on the left of the picture, the ruins of the Renaissance church of Santa María*

Renaissance elegance and style is the hallmark of Baeza's old quarter, where remnants of long years of Moorish influence have been replaced with 16th-century classical buildings of the highest order. The busy central Plaza de España extends into the tree-lined Paseo de la Constitución, with its lively pavement bars and cafés.

The town's Renaissance treasures lie on the higher ground, east of here. At the southern end of the Paseo de la Constitución is the handsome Plaza de los Leones, also known as Plaza del Pópulo, with its central fountain and double-arched gateway, the Puerta de Jaén.

Steps (Escalerillas de la Audienca) lead from the tourist office, then left to Plaza Santa Cruz, where you will find the Palace of Jabalquinto, with its superbly ornamented Gothic façade. The Renaissance courtyard and glorious baroque staircase are currently in poor condition, but are being refurbished. Opposite the palace is the delightful little Romanesque church of Santa Cruz, with traces of the earlier mosque that it supplanted.

The Cuesta de San Felipe leads uphill from Plaza Santa Cruz to Plaza de Santa María, the magnificent heart of Renaissance Baeza. The plaza is dominated by Baeza's massive 13th-century cathedral, which has an exhilarating 16th-century nave. At the centre of the square is a fountain in the form of a rustic triumphal arch, behind which stands the 16th-century seminary of San Felipe Neri, its walls bearing elegant graffiti.

BAÑOS DE LA ENCINA

This engaging little hilltop village rises from vast acres of olive fields. Baños has a lovely Gothic-Renaissance church in its tiny central Plaza de la Constitución, but the village is dominated by its well-preserved, 10th-century Moorish castle. The formidable custodian may be at the airy *mirador* on the way up to the castle; if not, ask at the Town Hall. You will be ushered through the double horseshoe arch into a huge central keep, where you can climb the Tower of Homage. Take care on the dark stairways: pigeons often explode into the light, and you may find pigeon's eggs perched mid-step. The views from the top are magnificent. Resist the challenge to walk round the inner, unprotected parapet if you do not have good footwork and a head for heights.

- 29D3
- 100km east of Córdoba
- Restaurante La Encina, c/ Ambulatorio 1 (€)
- Daily, Córdoba–Bailén, Úbeda–Bailén; local bus connections between Bailén and Baños
- Ayuntamiento
- Few

CAZORLA

The busy, unpretentious town of Cazorla, 'gateway' to the Parque Natural de Cazorla, Segura y Las Villas (► 13), nestles below the looming cliffs of the Peña de los Halcones. There is a lively daily market in Plaza del Mercado between the car park and c/Dr Muñoz, the main shopping street. Plaza de la Corredera, Cazorla's more sedate square, is surrounded by cafés and shops. From its far right-hand corner the narrow c/Nubla leads past the superb viewpoint of Balcón del Pintor Zabaleta, for fine views of Cazorla's ruined Moorish castle, La Yedra and its ruined Renaissance church of Santa María. Ruination apart, Plaza Santa María below the church, is a wonderful place to eat and drink.

- 29E3
- 32km southeast of Úbeda
- Cafés/restaurants (€–€€)
- Daily from Granada, Jaén and Úbeda
- Paseo del Santo Cristo 17 ☎ 953 71 01 02; c/Hilario Marco; Parque Natural Information Centre c/Martínez Falero 1 ☎ 953 72 01 25.
- Few
- Pilgrimage to La Virgen de la Cabeza, last Sun/Mon in Apr

Walk Along the Guadalquivir

Distance
2km

Time
1½ hours

Start/End point
Follow instructions for the Sierras drive (➤ 35) to turning at junction signed Coto Ríos; keep right here, signed Parador de Turismo and Vadillo Castril. At next junction keep left, signed Vadillo Castril. Soon, at a wide area, reach a junction with a road bending sharply right. Keep ahead for about 100m to a parking space on the right, just before a small house.

Lunch
Parador de Cazorla (€€€)
✉ Sierra de Cazorla s/n
☎ 953 72 70 75

The infant Río Guadalquivir at the heart of the Sierra de Cazorla

A short walk through dramatic mountain scenery alongside the infant Río Guadalquivir.

From the parking space, walk downhill to reach a bridge over the Río Guadalquivir. Turn left along a rocky path.

The Guadalquivir was first named Betis by the Romans, then Guad al Quivir (The 'Great River'), by the Moors. It rises in the heart of the Sierra de Cazorla and flows through Andalucía for 657km to the sea at Sanlúcar de Barrameda (➤ 73).

Follow the rocky path as it rises along the side of the river valley. Descend steeply and go down winding steps to reach a weir. Go down steps to the base of a waterfall that drops from the weir.

The valley widens here and is flanked on either side by great cliffs. Brightly coloured dragonflies and damselflies flit across the river pools.

Continue along the path beneath overhanging cliffs. There are shaded seats alongside the path.

Swifts dip and weave through the sky from their nests in the looming rocks above. Keep an eye open for mountain goats, which often graze at these lower levels.

Soon the path leads above a deep wooded valley and reaches a superb viewpoint just beyond an old well-head and water-pipe. Continue along a track through trees and keep left on the main track. At the next junction go right to reach a road and large parking area beside a notice board. Turn left and go downhill for a short distance to the parking space.

JAÉN ⭐

The provincial capital of Jaén lies in the middle of a bristling sea of olive trees: these have provided the city's staple product for centuries. Jaén is often given short shrift in terms of its appeal to the visitor. It is a pleasant enough city, however, though not as exotically Andalucían as other centres, in spite of long years of Islamic influence. Moorish moods still prevail in the old quarters of La Magdalena and San Juan, on the northeastern slopes of the Hill of Santa Catalina, and exploration of their streets is rewarding.

The scrub-covered Hill of Santa Catalina is crowned by the Castillo de Santa Catalina, its remnants transformed into a luxurious *parador* (state-run hotel). It is a stiff hike to the top of Santa Catalina, but the view from the cross-crowned *mirador* near the southern ruins is spectacular.

Down at street level, Jaén's main attraction is its vast and magnificent 16th-century cathedral. The west façade is a fine example of Renaissance baroque. The gloomy interior has an impressive display of great fluted Corinthian columns and rich carving. Other fine sights in Jaén include the Baños Árabes (Arab Baths), in the basement of the arts and crafts museum at the 16th-century Palacio de Villadompardo, just off Plaza San Blas. Another worthwhile visit can be made to the Museo Provincial in Paseo de la Estación. Collections from prehistory to Moorish and Renaissance times vie with the Museo de Bellas Artes (Museum of Fine Arts) upstairs, where there are some spectacularly bad but entertaining paintings, with provocative nudes in abundance as always.

29D3

90km east of Córdoba

Many bars, cafés and restaurants (€–€€€)

Paseo de la Estación
☎ 953 27 02 02

Plaza Coca de la Piñera
☎ 953 25 01 06

Calle de la Maestra 13
☎ 953 19 04 55;
www.aytojaen.es

Few

Semana Santa, San Lucas Fair, mid-Oct

Jaén Cathedral, a Renaissance masterpiece in stone

PRIEGO DE CÓRDOBA (▶ 23, TOP TEN)

SIERRAS DE CAZORLA SEGURA Y ❤❤❤
LAS VILLAS

The Sierras of Cazorla, Segura and Las Villas make up the largest of Andalucía's Parque Naturales (Natural Parks) at an impressive 214,000ha. The mighty Río Guadalquivir has its modest source here, amid spectacular rocky mountains that support great swathes of oak and pine woods. The Sierras are a complex of deep valleys and high ridges, with the mountain of Las Empanadas being the highest point at 2,107m. This is a winter landscape of snow and ice, but in late spring, summer and autumn the Sierras are delightful, often hot and sunny, yet verdant, with higher than average rainfall for such terrain. There are good opportunities for short or long walks, and you can also book trips on off-road Land Rovers.

There is a wealth of wildlife in these mountains. Over 1,000 plant species include the Cazorla violet, unique to the area. Trees include the black pine, Aleppo pine and evergreen oaks and there is a multitude of animals large and small, including fox, wild cat, polecat, otter, deer, mountain goat and wild boar. Birds include griffon vulture, booted and golden eagles, peregrine falcon and kite.

At Torre del Vinagre (▶ 35), 34km northeast of Cazorla, there is an **interpretation centre**. Adjoining the centre is a rather morgue-like Museo de Caza, a hunting museum, and nearby is a botanical garden. Land Rover trips and mountain bike or horse rides can be booked at the visitor centre.

✚ 29E3

✉ 90km northeast of Jaén

🍴 Bars, cafés and restaurants (€–€€)

🚌 Twice daily, Cazorla–Torre del Vinagre–Cotos Rios

ℹ C/ Arquitecto Bergés 1
☎ 953 22 27 37

ℹ Parque Natural Information Centre c/ Martinez Falero 11, Cazorla ☎ 953 72 01 25

♿ Few

Centro de Interpretación Torre del Vinagre

✚ 29E3

✉ Torre del Vinagre

☎ 953 71 30 40

🕐 Summer daily 10–2, 5–8:30; spring and autumn daily 11–2, 4–7; winter Tue–Sun 11–2, 4–6

The spectaclar ruin of the castle at La Iruela, near Cazorla, perched on a pinnacle of rock above the village

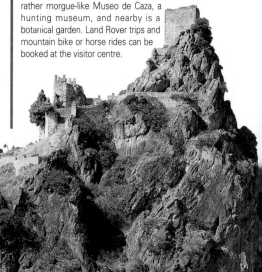

SEGURA DE LA SIERRA ⊕

The road to Segura has been greatly improved in recent years, yet it is still a challenging piece of tortuous driving to reach this charming and popular village. Segura and its Moorish castle perch on a 1,100m hill surrounded by peaks. The village is entered through a medieval gateway. Below the tiny village square of Plaza de la Encomienda is the Iglesia Nuestra Señora del Collado, a handsome little church with tiled roof and simple interior. Opposite the church is a superb Renaissance fountain, the Fuente Carlos V, complete with its own shoal of fish. Near the church is a well-preserved Arab bath house. Segura's castle has been much renovated over the years. You may need to ask for the key at the tourist office, but the castle gate is often open – a reward for the stiff climb past the Plaza de Toros, Segura's tiny bullring. The bullring looks overgrown and unused, but during Segura's October festival there is a *corrida* (bullfight); famous matadors, such as Enrico Ponce, have fought here. The view from the castle tower is outstanding, but take care on the often pitch-dark stairways.

ÚBEDA (► 25, TOP TEN)

ZUHEROS ⊕

The white houses of Zuheros cluster below a Moorish castle in the Sierra Subbética, in a world of cliffs and rocky bluffs. The village has a handsome church, the Iglesia de la Virgen de los Remedios, whose tower supplanted an earlier minaret. The narrow streets of Zuheros make for pleasant wandering, and are punctuated by fine viewpoints such as the Mirador de la Villa. East of Zuheros is the Cueva de los Murciélagos (Cave of the Bats), with prehistoric paintings. There are guided tours at weekends.

🗓 29E4
✉ 60km northeast of Úbeda
🕐 Open summer only
🍴 Casa Mesón Jorge Manríque (€€)
ℹ Paseo de Genaro Navarro
☎ 953 48 02 80
♿ Few
❓ Festivals: Santa Quiteria, 22 May; Santiago, 25 Jul; Virgen del Rosario, 5–8 Oct

The blue waters of Embalse de Tranco (Tranco Reservoir) are surrounded by the wooded hills of the Sierra de Segura

---

🗓 29D3
✉ 60km southeast of Córdoba
🍴 Mesón Atalaya, c/Santo 58 (€)
ℹ At entrance to village
☎ 957 69 47 75
♿ Few

Granada and Almería

The provinces of Granada and Almería contain Andalucía's most diverse landscapes. Granada province has the great mountain range of the Sierra Nevada at its heart, where the snow-streaked summit of Mulhacén rises above the green foothills of Las Alpujarras. Further east into Almería province, the green dwindles into an increasingly parched landscape of brown and ochre hills. Both provinces border the Mediterranean, where the holiday areas of the Costa de Almería and the Costa Tropical add to the variety. The city of Granada is famous for its spectacular Moorish Alhambra, one of the world's great architectural treasures, and Almería city boasts its own fortified Moorish palace, the Alcázaba.

The fascinating diversity of the two provinces extends to the towns and villages of the coast and interior, from the beach resort of Mójacar to the mountain villages of Trevélez and Capileira, and from the pottery villages of Nijar and Sorbas to the cave dwellings of Guadix.

> *'I will hasten from this prospect...before the sun is set. I will carry away a recollection of it clothed in all its beauty'*

Washington Irving, 1829

————————●————————

Above: *The Mexuar, the council chamber of the Alhambra's Casa Real*
Left: *the Renaissance style of Granada cathedral*

Granada

Granada stands at the foot of the Sierra Nevada massif, which acts as its dramatic backdrop. Dominating the town is the Alhambra (▶ 16–17), perched on its hilltop site facing the high ground of the Moorish quarter of Albaicín across the valley of the Río Darro. The Alhambra apart, there is much to see in Granada, from the stately cathedral to the remarkable buildings of the university quarter, and from the fashionable streets of the modern city to the bazaar-like alleyways linking the old city's delightful plazas.

Granada was the last stronghold of the Moors, the final jewel in the crown of the 15th-century Catholic Reconquest of Andalucía. From the early 8th century, the city was controlled from Moorish Córdoba, and then from Seville. In the 1240s Granada emerged as the capital of a separate and successful kingdom under the rule of an independent Arab prince of the Nasrid dynasty. Moorish Granada and its province survived intact for another two centuries until its final conquest in 1492 by Fernando and Isabel. Jealous of Moorish grandeur, they set a northern Spanish stamp on Granada, yet preserved the mighty Alhambra, the most spectacular of Andalucía's surviving Moorish monuments.

🛈 Corral del Carbón, s/n
☎ 958 22 59 90; www.
turismodegranada.es

Far left: *a fountain in the centre of Granada town*
Below: *A quiver of souvenir swords to draw on*

Left: *tourists examine the Mudéjar panelling of the Mexuar, the 14th-century council chamber of the Casa Real, the Royal Palace of the Alhambra*

45

What to See in Granada

THE ALBAICÍN ✪✪✪

44B2
Northeast of Plaza Nueva
Numerous bars and restaurants (€–€€)
Alhambrabus
Few

Below: *cooling off all round in Granada's Plaza Nueva*

Granada's antidote to its modern city streets is the engaging Albaicín, the old Moorish quarter that occupies the northern side of the valley of the Río Darro and the hill of Sacromonte, the city's much vaunted Gitano, or Gypsy quarter. The Albaicín is best reached from Plaza Nueva by following the Carrera del Darro, past the Baños Árabes (➤ 46) and the Museo Arqueológico (➤ 48) and on beyond the attractive terrace of Paseo de los Tristes, where there are numerous cafés in the shade of the Alhambra Hill. You can plunge into the heart of the Albaicín

by going along the Carrera del Darro and its continuation of Paseo del Padre Manjón, and then by turning left up Cuesta del Chapiz. Part of the way up, the Camino del Sacromonte leads off right into the Gypsy quarter and the notorious 'flamenco caves', where you risk off-loading large sums of money to watch insistent but not entirely authentic flamenco shows. The real pleasures of the Albaicín lie in the maze of streets and marvellous local plazas with their bars and restaurants. Find your way to the famous Mirador de San Nicolás for a world-famous sunset view of the Alhambra; but hang on to your bag, *very tightly*; the local thieves are absolute masters at spiriting away anything moveable the minute it is put down.

BAÑOS ÁRABES ✪

44B2
Carrera del Darro 31
Tue–Sat 10–2
Several in Paseo de los Tristes (€–€€)
Alhambrabus
Few
free

On the way along the Carrera del Darro from Plaza Nueva are the Baños Árabes (Arab Baths), a small but enchanting Moorish bathhouse, entered through a tiny courtyard garden with inlaid floor and tiny central pool. The 11th-century baths are well-preserved and have the typical star-shape and octagon-shape skylights in the roofs of their brick-vaulted chambers.

CAPILLA REAL ★★

The Capilla Real (Royal Chapel) was built between 1506 and 1521 as a sepulchre for Los Reyes Católicos, Fernando and Isabel, one of the most terrifying double acts in history. The Royal Chapel is an intriguing Gothic building, an odd mixture of the flamboyant and the constrained. It is impressive, yet lacks entirely the subtle elegance of Moorish buildings. Inside lies the Renaissance monument in Carrera marble, celebrating the two monarchs. Note how the head of Isabel's effigy is more deeply sunk into her pillow than Fernando's – a reflection, it is said, of her undoubtedly superior intelligence. Below the monument, down narrow steps, lie the lead coffins of the monarchs, their daughter Joana and her husband Felipe, although there is no certainty that they contain the genuine remains of anyone. The most striking feature of the chapel is the altar's superb *retablo* (alterpiece), a gilded extravaganza. In the sacristy are displayed, amongst royal heirlooms, Isabel's splendid collection of paintings by Flemish masters and others.

🪧 44A2
✉ Oficios 3
☎ 958 22 78 48
🕐 Apr–Oct Mon–Sat 10:30–1, 4–7, Sun 11–1, 4–7; Nov–Mar Mon–Sat 10:30–1, 3:30–6:30, Sun 11–1, 3:30–6:30
🍴 Bar-Restaurante Sevilla, c/ Oficios 12 (€€)
🚌 1, 3, 4, 6, 7, 8, 9
♿ Few
💰 Cheap

Above: *the mighty Renaissance columns of the Capilla Real*

CATEDRAL ★

Granada's cathedral stands near the apex of the busy junction of Gran Vía de Colón and Calle Reyes Católicos. The cathedral is crowded round by other buildings, but its massiveness and its stepped exterior of tiled turrets, gables and buttresses rising to a central dome dominate the cramped surroundings. The building dates from the 16th century and reflects all the contemporary certainties that raised it in place of a demolished mosque. The high central dome, supported on huge pillars, lends lightness to the interior and to the wealth of baroque chapels which can be illuminated at the drop of a coin in a switch box.

🪧 44A2
✉ Gran Vía de Colón 5
☎ 958 22 29 59
🕐 Mon–Sat 10:30–1:30, 4–7, Sun and public hols 4–7
🍴 Vía Colona, Gran Vía de Colón 13 (€€)
🚌 1, 3, 4, 6, 7, 8, 9
♿ Few
💰 Cheap

The lofty bell tower of the Convento de San Jerónimo overlooks a tree-shaded patio

➕ off map west
✉ Rector López Argueta 9
☎ 958 27 93 37
🕐 Apr–Oct Mon–Sat 10–1:30, 4–7:30, Sun 11–1:30, 4–7:30; Nov–Mar Mon–Sat 10–1:30, 3–6:30, Sun 11–1:30, 3–6:30
🍴 Numerous cafés in adjoining San Juan De Dios (€)
🚌 5
♿ Few 💷 Cheap

MONASTERIO DE SAN JERÓNIMO ✪

The 16th-century Convento de San Jerónimo (Convent of St Jeronimo) lies in the university district to the northwest of the cathedral. The focus of the convent is its central patio, a superb example of mixed Gothic-Renaissance features and with refreshingly peaceful cloisters, where the mellow chanting of the nuns at prayer can often be heard. The adjoining church has an inspiring interior, all painted frescoes and with a glorious four-storeyed *retablo* (altarpiece) within an octagonal apse.

The adjacent university district has a wealth of remarkable churches and secular buildings to offset the lively bustle of student life.

➕ Off map north
✉ Calle Real de Cartuja
☎ 958 16 19 32
🕐 Apr–Oct Mon–Sat 10–1, 4–8; Nov–Mar daily 10–1, 3:30–6:30
🚌 8 C
💷 Cheap

MONASTERIO DE LA CARTUJA ✪✪

The Monasterio de la Cartuja (Monastery of the Carthusians) lies some way from the city centre but is well worth the journey. It is the most extravagant of Spain's Carthusian buildings and dates from the early 16th century. The Cartuja's monastery and church face each other across an attractive patio. The church is a lavish torrent of baroque sculpture, all swirling marble and jasper and gilded frescoes.

➕ 44C2
✉ Carrera del Darro 41
☎ 958 22 56 40
🕐 Apr–Oct Tue 2:30–8, Wed–Sat 9–8,Sun 9–2:30; Nov–Mar Tue 2:30–6, Wed–Sat 9–6, Sun 9–2:30
🚌 Alhambrabus
♿ Few 💷 Cheap

MUSEO ARQUEOLÓGICO ✪

The Museo Arqueológico (Archaeological Museum) is located within a delightful Renaissance palace – the Casa de Castril. The building has a central patio from whose upper balcony you can see the Alhambra across a frieze of tiled roofs. A wide range of exhibits covers the prehistoric, Phoenician, Roman, Visigothic and Moorish periods and is made even more impressive by the elegant surroundings.

The Hills of Las Alpujarras

This drive links a number of charming villages along the winding roads of Las Alpujarras, the wooded slopes of the Sierra Nevada.

Leave Adra on the N340/E15; join the A347 at Junction 391, signed Berja. Bypass Berja and continue on the A347. In 12km, at a junction, go left (signed Ugíjar). Go through Ugíjar and follow signs for Valor and Yegen on the A348.

The road winds through wooded hills, with a delightful sense of remoteness and height. The English writer Gerald Brenan lived at Yegen during the 1930s and 40s; his book *South from Granada* gives a wonderful picture of Las Alpujarras.

Beyond Yegen pass Mecina Bombarón, then go right at the next junction. Pass through Juviles and then follow the rising road to reach another junction. Keep right and follow the GR421 to Trevélez. Leave Trevélez by the lower exit from the main square. Pass Pórtugos and Pitres and continue to Capileira in the scenic Poqueira Gorge (▶ 54). Retrace your route from Capileira for 2km, then go right at a junction; pass through Pampaneira and continue to Orgiva. At Orgiva centre, go right at traffic lights; follow a winding road, cross a bridge and go left onto the A348.

There are stunning views across the valley from the A348 to the Las Alpujarras foothills and the Sierra Nevada's highest peak, Mulhacén.

Pass Torvizcón and continue along the A348 to Cadiar. Follow signs for Yátor, then for Ugíjar. At Ugíjar, go right, signed Cherín and Berja. At the junction with A347, go right and continue past Berja to the N340/E15 and the junction to Adra.

Distance
170km

Time
10 hours

Start/End point
Adra
➕ 29E2

Lunch
Meson La Fragua (€€)
✉ c/ San Antoni 4, Trevélez
(near Hotel La Fragua)
☎ 958 85 86 26

Looking south towards the Sierra de Gádor from the high road through Las Alpujarras

49

What to See in Granada & Almería

ALHAMA DE GRANADA

Located on the lip of a rocky gorge Alhama de Granada has a down-to earth charm that complements its splendid old buildings. The town was a significant Moorish settlement due to its hot springs, the *al hamma*, which still attract devotees to the nearby Hotel Balneario (➤ 101). The town's main square, the Plaza de la Constitución, is a pleasant place in which to enjoy good *tapas* at surrounding bars.

The Moorish castle at the end of the lower square is privately owned. Near by is the Iglesia del Carmen, a handsome late-medieval church with a lovely stone fountain outside, its basins brimming with clear water. On the far side of the Iglesia del Carmen is a terrace overlooking the gorge of the Río Alhama. From the fountain in front of the church, walk with the gorge on your right, to c/Portillo Naveros, then go left up c/Baja Iglesia. Pass the charming Casa de la Inquisición, a small building with a perfect façade in the late Gothic/early Renaissance Plateresque style (the term refers to its similarity to silver-smiths' work). Then reach the pleasing little square, Plaza los Presos, and the handsome 16th-century Renaissance church of La Encarnación.

28D2

40km southwest of Granada

Café-Bar Andaluz, Plaza de la Constitución (€)

Granada – Alhama de Granada, every weekday

c/ Vendederas

☎ 958 36 06 86

Few

Alhama de Granada perched above its river gorge amidst pattered corn fields and olive groves

🅱 Parque San Nicolás
Salmerón
☎ 950 27 43 55;
fax 950 27 43 60

Almería

Almería was one of the great cities of Moorish Andalucía, rivalling Seville, but after the Christian Reconquest, the Spanish rulers neglected the port, and a series of earthquakes during the 16th century ruined large parts of the city. Today, Almería has great appeal as an essentially Spanish city with a distinctive North African flavour. Its most enduring monument is the renovated Moorish Alcazaba.

Modern Almería is divided into east and west by the Rambla de Belén, a wide boulevard that has thankfully replaced an unsightly dry river bed. West of the Rambla is the Paseo de Almería, an old-established and restored thoroughfare. Halfway down the Paseo, a broad alley leads to Almería's colourful morning market. At the north end of Paseo de Almería is Puerta de Purchena, the city's real focus, a busy junction groaning with traffic, but also bustling with life. Calle de las Tiendas running south from Puerta de Purchena, is one of Almería's oldest streets, now a fashionable shopping venue. Charming side streets lead via Plaza Flores and Torres Siloy to the Plaza San Pedro, with its handsome church and raised promenade.

Just west of Plaza San Pedro is the Plaza Vieja (Old Square), also known as the Plaza de la Constitución. This 17th-century arcaded square, a northern Spanish interloper to Moorish Almería, is entered through narrow alleyways. The central space is occupied by palm trees and a bone-white monument. On the west side is the theatrical façade of the Ayuntamiento (Town Hall).

29F2
Almanzor s/n
950 27 16 17
Daily 9–6:30
Few
Bar/café (€€)
Cheap; free with EU passport

LA ALCAZABA DE ALMERÍA

La Alcazaba dominates Almería, although the modern town seems oddly detached from it. The happily scruffy Barrio de Chanca, a district of brightly painted, flat-roofed houses, surges up to its walls. An entrance ramp winds steeply up to Puerta de las Justicia (the Justice Gate), unmistakeably Moorish in style. Beyond is the First Precinct, cleverly renovated and reflecting, in its gardens and water channels, what the original must have been like. The views over the city are superb. A gentle climb past flowering shrubs and tinkling water leads to a beautiful oasis of trees hard against the walls of the Second Precinct. Here marble slabs, inscribed with verses by García Lorca (► 14) and Fernando Villalon rest against the wall. Inside the Second Precinct are the foundations of Moorish bathhouses. The Third Precinct encloses the triangular fortress, originally Moorish but greatly strengthened by the Christians. The views are breathtaking. Across the broad valley of San Cristóbal to the west is the Mirador de San Cristóbal, linked to the Alcazaba by the Muralla de San Cristóbal, a distinctive fortified wall.

29F2
Plaza de la Catedral
Mon–Fri 10–5, Sat 10–1
Bodega Montenegro, Plaza Granero (22)
Parque de Nicolás Salmerón
Few
Cheap

Almería's Alcazaba above the Ermita de San Anton

CATEDRAL

Almería's cathedral seems more fortress than church. Its stark and formidable walls were built to repel the pirates and disaffected Moriscos (Christianised Jews) who haunted the coast in the aftermath of the Christian Reconquest. Look for the cheerful yet unexplained sun symbol on the east wall, at the entrance to the charming

> ### DID YOU KNOW?
>
> In Almería province numerous males are called Indalecio after the famous Indalo figure found in prehistoric cave paintings at the Letreros Caves near Velez Blanco. The Indalo is a stick figure of simple, yet expressive style. It has become an emblematic figure in Almería and features in numerous craft and souvenir items.

little Plaza Bendicho. The interior is fiercely Gothic and dark, but the choir has outstanding carved walnut stalls and there is a handsome 18th-century altar behind it. A door in the south wall leads to a sunny little Renaissance courtyard, brimming with shrubs and flowers.

LAS ALPUJARRAS (➤ 18, TOP TEN)

COSTA TROPICAL ★

The Costa Tropical is the westward extension of the Costa de Almería, and occupies Granada province's Mediterranean shoreline. It is less developed than its neighbour and has a stretch of spectacular rocky coastline, a number of pleasant beaches and attractive resorts such as Almuñécar and Salobreña. Almuñécar has some fine Phoenician, Roman and Moorish monuments. The resort's beaches are pebbly and cramped, but the stylish esplanade of Paseo Puerta del Mar makes up for this.

➕ 29E2
✉ Adra to Almuñécar
🍴 Numerous bars, cafés and restaurants in various towns and resorts (€–€€€)
🚌 Daily Almería–Málaga
♿ Few

GUADIX ★★

Guadix is noted for its splendid cathedral and for its remarkable 'cave' dwellings. The former dominates the heart of the town, its red sandstone walls hiding a darkly Gothic interior enlivened by baroque forms. Opposite the cathedral's main doorway is an archway leading to the Renaissance square of Plaza de la Constitución, known also as Plaza Mayor. From the square's far right-hand corner go up steps and along c/Sant Isteban to reach a cluster of handsome buildings including the Renaissance Palacio de Peñaflor and its neighbouring 16th-century church of San Augustín. Between the two there is a seminary, through which you gain entrance to the rather down-at-heel Moorish Alcazaba. To the left of the Palacio de Peñaflor, in a sunken square, is the church of Santiago, with a fine Plateresque door frame.

Walk north from the Alcazaba to reach the Barrio Santiago, Guadix's famous cave district, where remarkable dwellings have been carved out of the soft tufa of tall pinnacles. Visit the **Cueva Museo** (Cave Museum) for a good insight into the cave culture and lifestyle.

➕ 29E2
📍 60km east of Granada
🍴 Several bars, cafés and restaurants (€–€€)
🚌 Daily Granada–Guadix
🍴 Ctra. de Granada
☎ 958 66 26 65
♿ Few
❓ Fiestas Patronales de la Virgen de la Piedad, 6–15 Sep

Cueva Museo (Cave Museum)
➕ 29E2
✉ Plaza del Padre Poveda
🕐 Mon–Sat 10–2, 6–8, Sun 10–2, 4–6
🍴 Drinks kiosk (€)
🚌 Road train from town centre ☎ 958 66 35 57
♿ Few
💵 Cheap

The interior of a cave house in Guadix shows how the soft rock of the district can be excavated to create comfortable rooms

A Walk Along the Poqueira Gorge.

Distance
4.5km

Time
About 2 hours

Start/End point
Plaza Constitución, Capileira
➕ 29E2

Lunch
Bar El Tilo (€)
✉ Plaza Calvario, Capileira
☎ 958 76 31 81

This walk leads from Capileira through part of the dramatic gorge in the High Alpujarras.

Leave Capileira's main square from its bottom left-hand corner. Go towards the church tower then right down Cuesta Iglesia to Plaza Iglesia. Bear right downhill, then go right along c/ Placetilla. Bear left through a narrow section, pass a well, then keep right and go downhill. At the bottom of the slope, by an old balcony, go left and then right to a Parque Natural signpost.

The contrast between the dazzling white of the houses and the dark green of wooded slopes beyond is stunning.

Go right down hill; cross a footbridge and follow a track downhill, keeping left at a junction and descending quite steeply in places. At the bottom, go right at a junction and over a rocky section. In a few metres go down an earthy slope, then climb steadily through trees, keeping ahead and uphill at a junction.

The well-watered river valley of Poqueira reflects the rich vegetation of Las Alpujarras, a name which some believe derives from the Arabic phrase for 'hills of grass'.

Continue uphill above a small barn. At a junction keep left on the rocky path, then descend to a bridge across the Río Poqueira. Retrace your steps from the bridge to the previous junction. Take the left-hand branch. Follow the path to where it bends left between short walls. Turn right at the footpath sign and follow the good track round to the outskirts of Capileira. Follow the village street uphill to the main square.

Capileira nestles amongst the hills of Las Alpujarras

MOJÁCAR ★

There are two Mojácars, and both are busy places. The old hilltop town of Mojácar Pueblo is hugely popular with the large number of visitors to Mojácar Playa , the straggling beach-side development that dominates the nearby coast for several kilometres. Old Mojácar can still charm in spite of the pressure from relentless summer crowds. Fight your way out of the central Plaza Nueva and its airy viewpoint of Mirador de la Plaza Nueva, and climb left to the little garden of Plaza del Sol and then up to Plaza del Castillo for more exhilarating views. Head west from here to explore the narrow flower-bedecked streets and squares, with their excess of souvenir shops. After all this, the long narrow beaches of Mojácar Playa are easily reached.

29F2
65km northeast of Almería
Numerous bars, cafés, restaurants (€–€€)
Daily, Almería–Mojácar
Plaza Nueva
☎ 950 61 50 25
Few
Moors and Christian Fiesta, 10 Jun. Fiestas Patronales San Augustín, 25–30 Aug

MONTEFRÍO ★

This delightful village at the heart of olive-growing country is dominated by the Iglesia de la Villa, a splendid church on a craggy promontory. The other great building is the central Iglesia de la Encarnacíon, a circular neo-classical church, with a domed roof. Scores of swallows nests have created a remarkable frieze round the outside eaves. Montefrío is famous for its sausages, and there are several good bars and restaurants in which to sample them. There are also excellent local varieties of olives and olive oil. To the east of the village, along the road to Illora, is the Neolithic burial site of Las Peñas de los Gitanos, one of many prehistoric and Roman sites in the area.

29D2
35km northwest of Granada
Café Bar La Fonda, c/Amat 7(€)
Daily, Granada–Montefrío
None
Feria de Verano, 7–8 Jul. Fiestas Patronales, 14–17 Aug

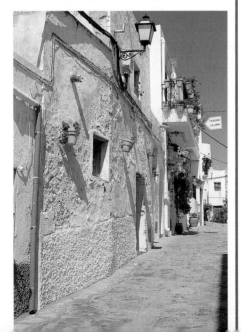

The streets of Mojácar wind in and out of sunlight and shade

In the Know

If you only have a short time to visit Andalucía and would like to get a real flavour of the city, here are some ideas:

10
Ways To Be A Local

Give serious thought to the siesta. Your time is precious on holiday, but the Spanish know what they are doing when they shut up shop and withdraw from the searing heat to the cool shade of patio and café-bar until 5 or 6.

Dress Spanish. It may go against holiday fashion, but if you want to 'be local' and if you do not want to be stared at, then do not wear shorts or scanty tops when visiting rural areas.

Enjoy evening drinks but be controlled. In Spain having several drinks too many, and showing it, is considered a sad indignity.

At local markets don't just sight-see. Get involved, sort through fabrics and clothes with intensity.

Identify locally favoured bars and cafés. Out of several café terraces in a plaza there is usually one full of local people.

Wear a sombrero with style. If you covet a 'straw hat', look for one in a village shop, where you'll pay much less than in big city gift shops.

Join in the evening paseo the relaxed stroll along avenue or promenade or around the plazas; and stop off for drinks and tapas on the way.

With meals, drink fino the deliciously cool dry sherry of the south. In Córdoba province never ask for fino, however. Instead drink the delicious local wine, montilla, a great rival to Jerez's vintage.

If you really want to be a local then go to a bullfight. If this is not to your taste go to a football match in one of the big cities for the experience of real Andalucían enthusiasm, or attend a religious festival such as Seville's Semana Santa or the pilgrimage to El Rocío (► 116) for a truly passionate Andalucían experience.

Accept that you can never be a local but get close to the experience by deferring to Spanish custom, by mastering a few courtesies in Spanish, and by appreciating the rich and complex character of the Andalucían people.

10
Good Places To Have Lunch

Bar Giralda (€–€€)
✉ Mateos Gago 1, Seville ☎ 954 22 74 35. One of the best tapas bars in Seville.

Cadiz (€)
✉ Plaza España ☎ 956 41 02 50. This pleasant little restaurant has an attractive courtyard for outdoor eating and offers good local dishes at reasonable prices. Game dishes when in season.

El Chinitas (€)
✉ Calle Moreno Monroy 4–6, Málaga ☎ 952 21 09 72. Popular tapas bar and traditional restaurant offering regional specialities.

El Portalon (€€€)
✉ Ctra. Cádiz, Km 178 ☎ 952 86 10 75. One of the coast's top-notch restaurants. Excellent selection of fresh seafood dishes and roast meats.

Left: siesta time
Above: a cart load of fashion in Seville

Gaitán (€€)

✉ Gaitán 3 ☎ 956 34 58 59. One of the most popular restaurants in town, with a good reputation for quality cooking. Rabo de toro a la Jerezana (bull's tail Jerez-style) features as one of its specialities.

Meson Diego (€)

✉ Plaza Constitución 12, Alhama de Granada ☎ 958 36 01 21. Great local bar-restaurant where you can sit outside and watch Andalucían life go by.

El Molino (€–€€)

✉ Plaza del Socorro 6, Ronda ☎ 952 87 93 32. Good terrace outlook on Ronda's busiest square. Good selection of main dishes and desserts.

La Parrala (€)

✉ Plaza de las Monjas 22, Moguer ☎ 959 37 04 52. Charming situation on the gleaming white Plaza de las Monjas, alongside the walls of the Convento de Santa Clara. Local gathering place in the evenings.

Siena (€)

✉ Plaza de las Tendillas, Córdoba ☎ 957 47 30 05. Well-placed café-restaurant for viewing life in the attractive Plaza de las Tendillas. Drinks, snacks, and *platas combinados*.

Via Colón (€€)

✉ Gran Via de Colon 13, Granada ☎ 958 22 98 42. Near the cathedral. Pleasant outside terrace. Snacks and local specialities.

Top Activities

Bird-watching. In spite of widespread shooting and other hazards, birds flock in and out of coastal Andalucía, especially in spring and autumn. The coastal nature parks are the places to be.

Football match. If there is a big match on, especially somewhere like Málaga, go along for the fantastic atmosphere.

Horse-riding. In the land of great horse-handling and riding, what else should you do?

People-watching. The ultimate activity. Choose a good café in a busy plaza or village square, morning or evening.

Scuba-Diving. Andalucía under water can be as spectacular as it can be on land.

Sightseeing. Everywhere, you will be spoiled for choice.

Swimming. The entire coast of Andalucía is yours to choose from, but look out for village and local swimming pools deep inland. They can be real life savers.

Tennis and golf. The Costa del Sol is the place for these sports. There are numerous courts and courses, although you may need to book well ahead and join a queue.

Walking. This is a rather non-Andalucían habit. But in the mountains, or along the more remote coastline, it is a glorious way of enjoying the country.

Windsurfing. Head for the Tarifa coastline of the Costa de la Luz for some of the best windsurfing conditions in the world.

Ready for take off: wind surfer at Tarifa

Top Souvenirs

Ceramic tiles or pots from Nijar, Sorbas, Úbeda or Seville.

Esparto ware from Úbeda.

Fino sherry from Jerez de la Frontera or Sanlúcar de Barrameda.

Flamenco costume and accessories from Seville.

Honey or pears in wine from Grazalema.

Top Markets

Almería: Aguilar de Campo. Daily exuberant food market.

Cádiz: La Libertad. Superb food market. Monday–Saturday mornings.

Cazorla: Plaza del Mercado, daily. Great place for local produce from the Sierras.

Córdoba: Plaza de Corderella, Saturday morning. General goods and marvellous atmosphere.

Órgiva: This western town of Las Alpujarras has a daily market with more than a hint of the 'alternative' culture introduced by northern European incomers.

🔲 29F2
✉ 30km northeast of Almería
🍴 Café Bar La Glorieta (€€)
🚌 Daily, Almería–Níjar
♿ Few

Inset: *the village fountain, Fuente de la Villa, at Níjar*
Main picture: *typical ceramic ware at Níjar*

NÍJAR ⭐

Ceramics and *jarapas*, light carpets and cloth goods, are specialities of this pleasant village at the foot of the Sierra Alhamilla. There are excellent pottery shops on Avda García Lorca, the broad main street, and in Barrio Típico Alfarero, leading off from the far end of García Lorca. As always in Andalucían villages, however, you need to go a little further to find the very special places. Walk on from the top of García Lorca past the tourist office and then up Calle Carretera to the church of Santa María de la Anunciación, which has an excellent Artesonado coffered ceiling (a panelled timber style of Moorish origin). Keep on to the left of the church, cross Plaza de Granero and continue up Calle Colón, past the covered market, to reach the wonderful Plaza del Mercado, with its overarching elm trees and striking Fuente de la Villa de Níjar, the blue-tiled public fountain with gaping fish-head faucets. Finally leave the top right-hand corner of the square to find, at Lavadero 2, La Tienda de los Milagros, (the 'Shop of Miracles') (▶ 107), selling some of the finest ceramic work you could hope to find.

🔲 29E2
✉ 35km
🍴 Several bars, cafés and restaurants (€–€€€)
🚌 Daily Granada–Solynieve
♿ Few

SOLYNIEVE (SIERRA NEVADA) ⭐

Solynieve (Sun and Snow), known previously as Pradollano, is Andalucía's bid for winter sports glory. The resort stands at 2,100m in fairly bleak surroundings, especially in summer. Winter conditions are boosted by scores of high pressure snow-makers and the resort has all the facilities of a modern ski centre.

SORBAS ⭐⭐

Sorbas is the village of the *casas colgadas*, the 'hanging houses', a picturesque term that sums up its dramatic clifftop location above a dry valley. There is a strong tradition of pottery-making: the main workshops are in the Barrio Alfarero, in the lower part of the village. The central square, the Plaza de la Constitución, is flanked by the church of Santa María and the old mansions of the dukes of Alba and Valoig. The plaza's central fountain sports the heads of fierce beasts, their mouths crammed with water faucets. As you wander through Sorbas, you will emerge at various *mirador* viewpoints above the cliffs. The village lies at the heart of the Parque Natural de Karst en Yesos, a dramatic limestone landscape. There are guided tours of the nearby **Cuevas de Sorbas** (Sorbas Caves).

- 🔲 29F2
- ✉️ 40km northeast of Almería
- 🍴 Café Bar Teide III, c/San Andrés 1 (€)
- 🚌 Daily, Almería–Sorbas
- ♿ Few
- ❓ Fiesta Cruz de Mayo, 1–3 May. Fiesta San Roque, 14–17 Aug

Cuevas de Sorbas
- 🔲 29F2
- ☎️ 950 36 47 04
- 💶 Expensive

VÉLEZ BLANCO ⭐⭐

The dramatically situated village of Vélez Blanco, in the Sierra Maria, is difficult to reach without your own transport. Its Renaissance castle seems to grow naturally from its rocky pinnacle, opposite the Sphinx-like mountain butte of La Muela. The castle is an extension of an original Moorish Alcazaba, and dates from the 16th century. Its sumptuous interiors were dismantled wholesale in 1904 after being sold to a dealer, and now languish in New York's Metropolitan Museum, but the castle still rewards a visit for its fine views, and the village is a delightful maze of streets with balconied houses and overhanging tiles. A short distance south are the Cuevas de los Letreros, where there are prehistoric cave paintings.

- 🔲 29F3
- ✉️ 30km north of Almería
- 🍴 Bar Sociedad (€)
- ♿ None

The Renaissance castle of Velez Blanco, built as an extension of a previous Moorish castle, or Alcazaba, dominates the view from miles around

Málaga and Cádiz

The provinces of Málaga and Cádiz are the most popular of Andalucían destinations – mainly because of Málaga's mass tourism venue, the Costa del Sol. Yet both provinces have some of the most remote inland and coastal areas in Andalucía. Málaga boasts the remarkable mountain areas of El Torcal (➤ 22) and the Sierra Ronda. The Atlantic coast of Cádiz has emptier beaches, and in the north of the province there are spectacular mountain areas, such as the Sierra de Grazalema.

Málaga city has outstanding monuments and a reassuring sense of everyday Andalucían life. Cádiz city has the same authenticity, with the extra magic of its sea-girt position and rich history. Fascinating provincial towns, such as Ronda and Jerez de la Frontera and a host of intriguing villages, add to the rich rewards offered by these most southerly provinces.

> *'...the bold features of the most*
> *picturesque country in Europe*
> *will afford recollections which*
> *I shall dwell upon with*
> *pleasure through the remainder*
> *of my life'*

William Jacob
Travels in the South of Spain, 1811

———————●———————

Left: *panoramic view of Málaga and its harbour from the heights of the Alcazaba and Gibralfaro*

i Pasaje de Chinitas 4
☎ 952 21 34 45

*Málaga's leafy
promenade*

Málaga

Málaga lies handsomely between the mountains and the sea. It is a busy, friendly city, relatively untouched by the conspicuous tourism of the crowded Costa del Sol, despite being the transit centre for most beach-bound visitors from Northern Europe. The city has lost some of its style through excessive development, but its major monuments, such as the Moorish Alcazaba and its subdued but intriguing cathedral, survive. Many historic buildings have been restored. Beautiful churches, the new Museo Picasso and other fine museums, fashionable shops, an excellent mix of bars and restaurants and a persuasive Mediterranean climate all add to Málaga's charm.

Málaga city lies on either side of the Río Guadalmedina, an arid trench for most of the summer. To its west lie large swathes of modern development and what is left of the old district of El Perchel. East of the river, the broad, tree-lined avenue Alameda, the main axis of the city and home to numerous flower stalls, leads to the busy traffic junction of Plaza de la Marina. Beyond it is the delightful Paseo del

Parque, a palm-shaded promenade complete with a botanical garden and lined with fine buildings. Look for the bronze sculpture, *The Jasmine-Seller*, as you stroll in the mellow Málaga evening.

South of the Alameda, a dense block of buildings robs the main city of views to the harbour and to the sea. North of the avenue is the commercial centre, where the area round the market on Calle Atarazanas preserves much of the atmosphere of the old city. East of here are the busy shopping streets that radiate from the lively and diverting Plaza de la Constitución, from which the main street of Calle Larios links the centre with Plaza de la Marina. Scattered throughout the main centre are numerous bars and restaurants, where you can enjoy Malaga's distinctive cuisine, including its famous fried fish. A few steps east from Plaza de la Constitución take you to the attractive streets and plazas of the historic cathedral district. Above the city is the Alcazaba on its stepped hill that rises even higher to the Castillo de Gibralfaro.

Refreshing view of the Alcazaba

What to See in Málaga

LA ALCAZABA ✪✪✪

Málaga's Alcazaba has a wonderful sense of antiquity in its rough walls and in the maze of terraces, gardens, patios and cobbled ramps that lead ever upwards through impressive archways into the sunlight. The lower part of the Alcazaba dates from the 8th century, but the main palace is 11th-century. Málaga's long history is reflected in the partly excavated Roman theatre, below the entrance to the Alcazaba, and in the various marble classical columns embedded within the dark brickwork of the fortress. The upper palace contains the small Museo de la Alcazaba which displays Moorish artefacts recovered from the site and vicinity, amid decorative patios and rooms. Views of Málaga from the ramparts of the Alcazaba are magnificent.

➕ 29D2
✉ c/ Alcazabilla s/n
☎ 952 21 60 05
◉ Museo de la Alcazaba
  Tue–Sun 8:30–7
🍴 El Jardín, c / Canon 1
  (€–€€)
🚌 35
♿ None
💶 inexpensive

CASA NATAL DE PICASSO ✪

🚩 29D2
✉ Plaza de la Merced 15
☎ 952 06 02 15
🕐 Mon–Sat 10–8, Sun 10–2
🍴 Several cafés in Plaza de la Merced (€)
♿ Few
💶 Free

You cannot fault a city whose most famous son was one of the world's greatest painters, Pablo Ruiz y Picasso (1881–1973). The Casa Natal Picasso (Picasso's Birthplace) is the headquarters of the Picasso Foundation, and is located in a handsome terrace of 19th-century houses in the large and friendly Plaza de la Merced, with its big central memorial. The building is significant more for its sense of Picasso's presence than for its rather spare (though elegant) rooms, converted out of Picasso's early home. There are some fine mementoes and photographs of the artist, not least the striking photograph in the entrance foyer.

CASTILLO DE GIBRALFARO ✪

🚩 29D2
✉ Monte del Faro
🕐 Daily 9–6
🍴 Parador de Málaga Gibralfaro (€€€)
🚌 35 from Paseo del Parque. Horse–drawn carriages also make the trip from the Paseo del Parque and from outside the cathedral
♿ Few
💶 Inexpensive

The much-renovated Moorish Castillo de Gibralfaro (Castle of Gibralfaro) stands high above Málaga and above the Alcazaba, to which it is connected by a parapet wall. There

The sturdy walls of the Castillo de Gibralfaro. The name Gibralfaro derives from the phrase 'rock of the lighthouse' and relates to ancient times when a lighthouse stood on the hilltop

are exhilarating views from the ramparts and from the terraced approach path, that leads you up from the Alcazaba amidst a deluge of bougainvillea and flower beds – but hang on to your wallet or handbag.

CATEDRAL ✪

Málaga's cathedral gets something of a bad press, due perhaps to its lack of a companion for its solitary tower. Another tower was planned originally, but was never constructed. The cathedral has a strong visual appeal, however, its dark, worn stonework making a pleasing contrast to the more modern buildings that crowd round it. Inside there is much Gothic gloom, in heavily marbled surroundings, with numerous attractive side chapels competing for attention. The coro, or choir, is the cathedral's great glory: its fine mahogany and cedar wood stalls are embellished by carved statues of 40 saints. The adjoining church, the Iglesia del Sagrario, has a Plateresque doorway and a Renaissance high altar that will take your breath away.

🗺 29D2
✉ c/Molina Larios s/n
☎ 952 21 59 17
🕐 Cathedral: Mon–Sat 10–6:45. Closed Sun. Iglesia del Sagrario: daily 9:30–12:30, 6–7:30
🍴 El Jardín, c/ Canon 1 (€–€€)
♿ Few
🎟 Cheap

MUSEO DE ARTES Y TRADICIONES POPULARES ✪✪

This excellent museum is located in a restored 17th-century inn, the Mesón de la Victoria, built round a little courtyard. On display is a host of traditional artefacts from the rural and seagoing life of old Málaga province, a rich reminder of a less frenetic age.

🗺 29D2
✉ c/Pasillo de Santa Isabel 10
☎ 952 21 71 37
🕐 Summer Mon–Fri 10–1, 5–8. Sat 10–1. Rest of year Mon–Fri 10–1:30, 4–7, Sat 10–1. Closed Sun and public hols
🍴 El Corte Inglés Buffet Grill (€), Avenida de Andalucía
♿ Few
🎟 Cheap

The green and leafy central courtyard of the Museo de Artes Y Tradiciones Populares

MUSEO PICASSO ✪✪

The long-awaited Picasso Museum finally opened in October 2003. Housed in the handsome 16th-century Palacio de Buenavista, this splendid new museum contains a collection of more than 200 Picasso works including paintings, drawings, sculptures, engravings and some fine ceramics. Some archaeological remains can be viewed in the basement.

🗺 29D2
✉ Palacio de Buenavista, Calle San Agustin 8
☎ 902 44 33 77
🕐 Tue–Thu 10–8, Fri, Sat 10–9
🎟 Moderate

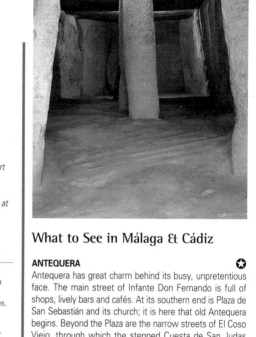

Sturdy uprights support the roof of the Menga Bronze Age burial chamber, or 'dolmen', at Antequera

What to See in Málaga & Cádiz

ANTEQUERA ⊕

Antequera has great charm behind its busy, unpretentious face. The main street of Infante Don Fernando is full of shops, lively bars and cafés. At its southern end is Plaza de San Sebastián and its church; it is here that old Antequera begins. Beyond the Plaza are the narrow streets of El Coso Viejo, through which the stepped Cuesta de San Judas leads to the Arco de los Gigantes, a 16th-century gateway to the Plaza Santa María and its church, with a handsome Plateresque façade. There are exhilarating views from here of the town and countryside. Steps lead from the Plaza to the ruined Moorish Alcazaba. On Antequera's northeastern outskirts, on the Granada road, is a group of impressive Neolithic—Bronze Age burial chambers, the Menga and Viera **Dolmens**.

ARCOS DE LA FRONTERA ⊕

Arcos de la Frontera is one of Andalucía's liveliest towns. It has outgrown its Moorish hilltop settlement and now spills down from the craggy heights in a long, straggling tail of white buildings above the flat plain of the Río Guadalete. The older, upper part of Arcos is a maze of narrow streets that twist and turn round the two main churches of Santa María de la Asunción and San Pedro. The former dominates the central square of Plaza del Cabildo, from whose *mirador* there are stunning views of the plain below. Arcos has several other fine buildings, but the greatest reward comes from wandering through the old quarter and enjoying the everyday life of the lower town in Calle Corredera and the broad Paseo de Andalucía.

✚ 28C2
✉ 38km north of Málaga
🍴 Several (€–€€)
🚌 Estación de Autobuses, Campillo Alto s/n
☎ 952 70 35 73
🛈 Plaza San Sebastian 7
☎ 952 70 25 05
♿ Few
Dolmens
✚ 28C2
✉ Off Camino del Cementerio
🕐 Tue 3–5:30, Wed–Sat 10–1, 4–8, Sun, pub hols 10–2. Closed Mon
🎟 Free

✚ 28B2
✉ 50km northeast of Cádiz
🍴 Numerous bars, cafés and restaurants (€–€€€)
🚌 Daily, Cádiz–Arcos, Jerez de La Frontera–Arcos
🛈 Plaza del Cabildo
☎ 956 70 22 64
♿ Few
❓ Holy Week. Easter bull-running. Feria de San Miguel, end Sep

Cádiz

Cádiz captivates without even trying. This is one of the great historic ports of the Mediterranean, with a claim to being the oldest of European cities, and a distinctive peninsular site lending it immense character. The city was founded as *Gaadir* by the mineral-seeking Phoenicians, who exploited the tin and copper of the Sierra Morena. Under later Moorish control the city declined, and even today that distinctive Andalucían Moorishness seems absent from Cádiz. During the 18th century, the decline of Seville as a river port benefited Cádiz and the city became rich on the Spanish-American gold and silver trade.

Today there is a refreshing sense of easy-going life in the city's maze of streets and squares and along the great sweep of its breezy sea-front promenades. Tall buildings, salt-eroded and dark-stoned, enclose narrow, shaded alleys that open suddenly into great sun-drenched plazas and gardens and to the glittering Mediterranean. the main square of Plaza San Juan de Dios, with its handsome Ayuntamiento (Town Hall), and its encircling bars and cafés, makes a lively introduction; and the morning market in Plaza de La Libertad is a blur of colour and movement. The city's splendid churches and museums, its fashionable shops and fine restaurants, its beaches and its flower-decked gardens all combine to make Cádiz a unique experience – even for Andalucía.

🎯 28B2
ℹ️ Avenida Ramón de Carranza, s/n
☎ 956 25 86 46;
www.guiadecadiz.com

The domes of Cádiz's massive cathedral dominate the city skyline

Cádiz seafood displays are works of art in themselves

What to See in Cádiz

CATEDRAL NUEVA ✪

The massive Catedral Nueva (New Cathedral) is still under restoration but open to the public. The building dates from the prosperous 18th century, and replaced the 'old' cathedral of Santa Cruz. The neo-classical main façade on Plaza de la Catedral is magnificent. It is crowned by a baroque dome, famously 'gilded' yet, in reality, faced with glazed yellow tiles. The interior of the cathedral is a gaunt, stone cavern, classically perfect; below lies the claustrophobic crypt, which contains the grave of the musician Manuel de Falla (➤ 14).

<table>
<tr><td>✚</td><td>28B2</td></tr>
<tr><td>⊠</td><td>Plaza de la Catedral</td></tr>
<tr><td>🕓</td><td>Tue–Sat 10–12:30 (check with tourist office during refurbishment)</td></tr>
<tr><td>🍴</td><td>Café Bar La Marina, Plaza de las Flores (€€)</td></tr>
<tr><td>🚌</td><td>4</td></tr>
<tr><td>♿</td><td>Few</td></tr>
<tr><td>💷</td><td>Moderate</td></tr>
</table>

MUSEO DE CADIZ ✪✪✪

The Museo de Cadiz (Cadiz Museum) is the pride of Cádiz and one of the best museums in Andalucía. The ground-floor collection is outstanding, especially the Roman displays. On the first floor are paintings by Roger van der Weyden, Murillo, Rubens and Zurbarán, and the top floor has displays of craftwork and a bewitching collection of traditional marionettes.

<table>
<tr><td>✚</td><td>28B2</td></tr>
<tr><td>⊠</td><td>Plaza de Mina 5</td></tr>
<tr><td>☎</td><td>956 21 22 81</td></tr>
<tr><td>🕓</td><td>Tue 2:30–8, Wed–Sat 9–8, Sun 9:30–2:30</td></tr>
<tr><td>🍴</td><td>Cervecería Gaditana, C/Zorilla (€€)</td></tr>
<tr><td>🚌</td><td>2</td></tr>
<tr><td>♿</td><td>Few</td></tr>
<tr><td>💷</td><td>Cheap; free with EU passport</td></tr>
</table>

ORATORIO DE SAN FELIPE NERI ✪✪

Of all Cádiz's churches the Oratorio de San Felipe Neri is the most impressive. In March 1812 the building saw the temporary setting up of the Spanish parliament, or Cortes, that proclaimed the first Spanish Constitution – a radical document whose liberal principles were to influence European politics as a whole. Plaques on the outer wall commemorate leading Cortes deputies. Inside, two tiers of

balconies above exuberant chapels complement the high altar and its Murillo painting, *The Immaculate Conception*, all beneath a sky-blue dome.

The nearby **Museo Iconográfico e Histórico** (Iconographic and Historical Museum) has a marvellous scale model of the late 18th-century city, carved in wood and ivory.

One of the vivid statues in the church of San Felipe Neri

<table>
<tr><td>✚</td><td>28B2</td></tr>
<tr><td>⊠</td><td>Calle Santa Inés 38</td></tr>
<tr><td>☎</td><td>956 21 16 12</td></tr>
<tr><td>🕓</td><td>Mon–Sat 10–1:30</td></tr>
<tr><td>🍴</td><td>Freiduría Las Flores, Plaza de las Flores (€€)</td></tr>
<tr><td>🚌</td><td>2</td></tr>
<tr><td>♿</td><td>Few</td></tr>
<tr><td>💷</td><td>Cheap</td></tr>
</table>

Museo Histórico Municipal

<table>
<tr><td>✚</td><td>28B2</td></tr>
<tr><td>⊠</td><td>c/ Santa Inés 9</td></tr>
<tr><td>☎</td><td>956 22 17 88</td></tr>
<tr><td>🕓</td><td>Jun–Sep Tue–Fri 9–1, 5–8, Sat and Sun 9–1; Oct–May Tue–Fri 9–1, 4–7, Sat and Sun 9–1</td></tr>
<tr><td>🍴</td><td>Café Bar La Marina, Plaza de las Flores (€)</td></tr>
<tr><td>🚌</td><td>2</td></tr>
<tr><td>♿</td><td>Few</td></tr>
<tr><td>💷</td><td>Cheap</td></tr>
</table>

A Stroll Through Old Cádiz

A walk through the narrow streets of the old town, visiting museums and one of Cádiz's most remarkable churches on the way.

From the far corner of the Plaza San Juan de Dias, to the right of the Town Hall, go along c/ Pelota and into Plaza de la Catedral. Leave by the far right hand corner of the Plaza and go along Compaña to the busy Plaza de la Flores. Leave the Plaza to the left of the post office building to reach the market square, La Libertad.

Distance
2.5km

Time
About 3 hours, with visits to museums and churches

Start/End point
Plaza San Juan de Dios

Lunch
El Madrileño (€–€€)
✉ Plaza de Mina

Plaza de la Flores is surrounded by fine buildings overlooking a flower market. The food market in La Libertad is in full swing in the mornings.

Leave the market square along Hospital de Mujeres. Turn right along Sagasta and continue to Sta Ines. Go left here and pass the Museo Iconográfico e Histórico to reach the Oratorio de San Felipe Neri (➤ 68). From the church go down San José crossing junctions with Benjumeda and Cervantes, then left through Junquería into Plaza de San Antonio.

This vast square edged with seats is a pleasant place to relax in the sunshine.

Cádiz is a beautiful maze of shaded streets and sunlit plazas

Leave the Plaza on the same side as you entered, but go down Ancha, then go left along San José to Plaza de Mina and the Museo de Bellas Artes y Arqueológico (➤ 68). Take Tinte, to the right of the museum, to Plaza de San Francisco. From the Square's opposite corner follow San Francisco through Plaza de San Augustín and on down Calle Nueva to Plaza San Juan de Dios.

29D1

Between Málaga and Gibraltar

Enormous number of bars, cafés and restaurants (€–€€€)

Regular service from Málaga to all resorts

Regular service Málaga–Torremolinos–Fuengirola

Inset: *one of Gibraltar's famous features, a Barbary ape*
Main picture: *unmistakable Gibraltar*

28C1

120km southwest of Málaga

Several bars, cafés and restaurants (€€–€€€)

Daily, Cádiz–La Linea, Málaga–La Linea; regular buses La Linea–Gibraltar

Good

COSTA DEL SOL ✪

Conspicuous tourism is the business of the Costa del Sol, the long ribbon of holiday development that runs from Nerja, east of Málaga, along its western shore to Manilva. A sun-seeking break on the Costa has been the aim of millions of tourists over the years and the Costa has responded with gusto. Main resorts such as Marbella and Puerto Banús have an upmarket image to match prices, while the middle-range resorts of Torremolinos, Fuengirola, Benalmádena Costa and Estepona cover a range of styles from 'outgoing' to 'retiring'. All sum up the sea, sun, sand and sangría image. Smaller resorts, such as Sotogrande and San Pedro de Alcántara, now merge with the seamless concrete of the Costa. You will find more Englishness than Andalucían here, but for a good beach holiday, the Costa del Sol is still hard to beat.

GIBRALTAR ✪

The wide open spaces of the airport approach to Gibraltar emphasise just how spectacular the famous 'Rock' is. This is the genuine point of contention between Spain and Britain, steeped in nautical history. Gibraltar has been a British colony since 1704 and, although its populace has evolved into an engaging mix of British-Mediterranean character, the buildings, culture, style and especially the commerce are emphatically British. There is enough in Gibraltar to make a visit enjoyable apart from the fascination of the mighty rock: its famous apes, the cable car, St Michael's Cave and views to Africa. Passports must be shown at the police and customs post.

View across the rooftops of Grazalema at the heart of the Sierra de Grazalema, a magnificent area of wooded mountains

GRAZALEMA ⊙⊙

Mountains define Grazalema. They loom like clouds above the village and fill the distant horizon. This is the heart of the Parque Natural Sierra de Grazalema (➤ 12), a spectacular area of harsh limestone peaks softened by vast swathes of the rare Spanish fir, the Pinsapo, as well as by cork oak and holm oak. The impressive peak of San Cristóbal towers above Grazalema. In the charming central square, the Plaza de Andalucía, is the attractive church of Nuestra Señora de la Aurora. There is a fountain with amusing faucet heads to the side of a little lane called Agua, which leads to a flower-filled patio ringed by café–restaurants. The craft shop above the tourist office sells high quality, locally made clothes and produce.

🔷 28C2
✉ 20km west of Ronda
ℹ Plaza de España
☎ 956 13 22 25
🍴 Cádiz El Chico, Plaza de España (€€)
🚌 Daily, Ronda–Grazalema
♿ Few
❓ Feria de Grazalema 22–25 Aug

JEREZ DE LA FRONTERA (➤ 20, TOP TEN)

MEDINA SIDONIA ⊙

Nothing could be more detached from seagoing than this quiet hilltop town, yet Medina Sidonia was the ducal home of the admiral who led the Spanish Armada in its disastrous attack on Britain. The tree-lined main square, the Plaza de España, is overlooked by the Ayuntamiento (Town Hall). At a shop here, or at the Convento de San Cristóbal in c/ Hercules 1, you can buy some of Medina's famous *dulces* (sweet cakes), such as the almond-flavoured *alfajores*. In the upper town, the church of Santa María la Coronada, in the sunny Plazuela de la Iglesia Mayor, has a very fine altarpiece; behind it are the remains of a Moorish Alcazar. From the Plazuela, a path leads to hilltop views of the surrounding countryside of La Janda.

🔷 28B1
✉ 30km east of Cadíz
🍴 Mesón Bar Machin, Plaza Iglesia Mayor 9 (€€)
🚌 Daily, Cadíz–Medina Sidonia, Mon–Fri
♿ Few

Above right: *Ronda's gorge spanned by the Puente Nuevo*
Above inset right: *Ronda's bullring during the September Feria*
Right: *Nerja's famous Balcon de Europa*

NERJA ✪✪
These days Nerja is firmly established as part of the Costa del Sol, which now lies officially within the province of Málaga. It is an enjoyable though busy resort with pleasant beaches, and is famed for its Balcón de Europa, a palm–lined promontory on the old belvedere of an original fortress. There is an appealing freshness about Nerja but the form of the old town survives in its narrow streets. It can be crowded, however, especially at weekends, but it maintains a relaxed air. The cool interior of the simple church of El Salvador by the Balcón de Europa reflects this detachment. The best beaches, Calahonda and Burriana, lie to the east of the Balcón. The popular limestone caves, the **Cuevas de Nerja**, lie about 4km east of the village.

RONDA ✪✪
The dominant feature of picturesque Ronda is the deep gorge (El Tajo) of the Río Guadalevín. Between its towering walls a handsome 18th-century bridge, the Puente Nuevo, hangs like a wedge, groaning beneath the massed weight of visitors. On the south side of the bridge is the old Moorish town, largely sanitised but still charming. Its focus is the Plaza Duqueza de Parcent, where the fine Iglesia de Santa María Mayor stands on the site of an original mosque. The church has strong Gothic and baroque features, but numerous Moorish elements survive to add an exotic flair. Other places to visit south of the gorge include the nearby Palacio de Mondragón in c/ Manuel Montero, the Minaret de San Sebastian in c/ Armiñan, the Iglesia del Espíritu Santo close to the Puente Nuevo and the well-preserved Arab Baths near the Puente Viejo, or Old Bridge, to the east.

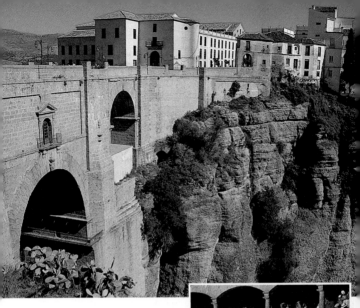

On the north side of the Puente Nuevo is the Mercadillo district of modern Ronda. Halfway along c/Virgen de la Paz is Ronda's famous bullring, opened in 1785 and an architectural joy. It was here that Pedro Romero established the intricate rules of fighting bulls on foot. The attached museum is full of bullfighting memorabilia, but it is the golden circle of blinding sand and the rough but elegant stonework of the tiers of covered seats that captivate. From opposite the bullring, stroll up Carrera Espinel, the pedestrianised main shopping street, where you will be spoiled for choice.

SANLÚCAR DE BARRAMEDA ☆

Brace yourself for Barrameda. This is a lively seaside town, where life is washed down with *manzanillas*, a deliciously dry sherry touched lightly by the sea air, and the seafood is renowned. Sanlúcar is located at the mouth of the Río Guadalquivir, and was a leading port in the 16th century, associated with the voyages of Columbus and Magellan. Its 16th-century prosperity bequeathed a number of decaying but still handsome Renaissance churches and buildings. The central, palm–lined square of Plaza de Cabildo has numerous bars and restaurants and the adjoining Plaza de San Roque is enlivened even more by the adjacent market. Sanlúcar's beaches are not the most salubrious, but exciting horse races are staged regularly on the long stretches of sand.

✚ 28B2
✉ 82km south of Seville, 36km north of Cádiz
ℹ Calzada del Ejército s/n
☎ 956 36 61 10
🍴 Numerous bars, cafés and restaurants (€–€€€)
🚌 Daily, Cádiz–Sanlúcar, Jerez–Sanlúcar, Seville–Sanlúcar
♿ Few
❓ Feria de la Manzanilla, last week of May. Horse-racing festival mid-Aug. Guadalquivir Festival, 23–25 Aug

A Drive Through the Pine Mountains

Distance
85km

Time
Six hours, with stops

Start/End point
Ronda
➕ 28C2

Lunch
Marqués de Zahara (€–€€)
✉ c/San Juan 3, Zahara de la Sierra
☎ 956 12 30 61

A short drive from Ronda through the spectacular mountain roads of the Parque Natural Sierra de Grazalema.

Leave Ronda, following signs to Seville. Join the A376 and in about 15km turn left onto the A372. After about 1.5km turn left; at the next junction, turn right (signed Grazalema).

The road winds down towards the village past overhanging roadside crags where you may see rock-climbers inching their way up the smooth faces.

Continue through Grazalema and in a few kilometres turn off right at a junction (signed Zahara de la Sierra).

On the road to Grazalema

This spectacular mountain road through the Sierra Margarita climbs to the Puerta de Palomas Pass, at 1357m. The mountains are covered in a mix of Pinsapo pine, a rare species found only in the Grazalema area, cork oak and holm oak. You may see an eagle drifting over the high ground.

Once over the pass, the road follows a series of spectacular hairpin bends that demand concentration, especially since the views are spectacular. At Zahara de la Sierra (▶ 26), drive as far as the central square, go round its central point then bear right and follow narrow streets downhill through the one-way system. At the bottom of the hill turn right and at a junction, right again. Follow the edge of the Embalse de Zahara (Zahara Reservoir). At a junction with the road to Grazalema, keep left; at the next junction, turn left. At a junction with the A376, turn right and return to Ronda.

TARIFA ✪

Tarifa is Europe's most southerly point. Africa is within reach: the blurred outlines of the Moroccan mountains loom across the Strait of Gibraltar only 14km away. It was at Tarifa, not surprisingly, that the Moors gained a first foothold on *al-Andalus* in 710. Tarifa is often swept by fierce winds from the stormy bottleneck of the Strait, where Mediterranean and Atlantic meet head-on. Today, the once remote beaches of Tarifa have been reinvented as world-class venues for windsurfing. You can dodge the wind amid the wriggling lanes and tiny squares and patios of Tarifa's walled Moorish quarter where, in Plaza de San Mateo, the 15th-century Iglesia de San Mateo has a glorious Gothic interior with rich baroque elements. Head west from Tarifa to some of the finest, if often breeziest, beaches around, or visit the impressive Roman ruins at **Baelo Claudio,** 14km along the coast towards Cádiz.

✚ 28B1
✉ 90km southeast of Cádiz
ℹ Paseo de la Alameda s/n
☎ 956 68 09 93;
www.tarifaweb.com
🍴 Numerous bars, cafés and restaurants (€–€€€)
🚌 Daily, Málaga–Tarifa, Cádiz–Tarifa
♿ Few
❓ Fiesta de la Virgen de la Luz, 6–13 Sep

Baelo Claudio
✚ 28B1
✉ Bolonia s/n
☎ 956 68 85 30
🕐 Guided visits, daily, Jul–mid-Sep 10, 11, 12, 1, 5, 6; Mid-Sep–Jun 10, 11, 12, 1, 4, 5, Sun, pub hols, 10, 11, 12
♿ Few
✋ Cheap; free with EU passport

Vejer de la Frontera, one of Andalucía's most vividly Moorish towns

VEJER DE LA FRONTERA ✪

More than most Andalucían Moorish towns and villages, Vejer is where you come close to the haunting memory of Arabic *al-Andalus*. The symbol of the woman wearing the *cobija*, the dark veiling cloak of the Moors, remains as a token of Vejer's remote hilltop location and its enchanting maze of narrow streets and buildings. The attractive 19th-century tiled fountain in the main square of Plaza de España represents a much later Spain. Vejer de la Frontera is meant for wandering through at will, discovering such features as the old Moorish castle and the 16th-century church of Divino Salvador.

✚ 28B1
✉ 42km southeast of Cádiz
🍴 Numerous bars, cafés and restaurants (€–€€)
🚌 Daily, Málaga–Cádiz, Cádiz–Vejer. Cadiz buses go to Vejer; Málaga–Cádiz buses stop on main road below village. From here, 4km steep walk, or taxi from nearby bars
♿ Few
❓ Easter Sun, bull-running. Fiestas de la Virgen

ZAHARA DE LA SIERRA (► 26, TOP TEN)

Seville and Huelva

Andalucía's most westerly provinces of Sevilla (Seville) and Huelva are precisely defined by the hills of the Sierra Morena in the northwest and by the fertile plain of the Río Guadalquivir, La Campiña, in the south-east. The Sierra Morena is the least-populated part of Andalucía, and although these hills lack the spectacular ruggedness of other ranges, their tree-covered slopes and scattered villages have an appealing remoteness. The region's coastline is contained mainly within Huelva province and includes the great delta of the Guadalquivir and the Parque Nacional Coto de Doñana (► 12)

Seville lies at the heart of the region. This is Andalucía's capital and its most fashionable city, home to magnificent monuments and with a cultural life to match any city in Europe. Huelva city is a more mundane, workaday place, fuelled by industry, but with some fine churches and museums.

> *'Who brought down the cool waters from rocky prisons, turning whole wastes into sunny vineyards and gardens? The Moors'*

Matilda Betham
Through Spain to the Sahara, 1868

———————•———————

Left: *sightseeing in style in Seville's Plaza de España*
Above: *brilliant flowers grace Seville's Casa de Pilatos*

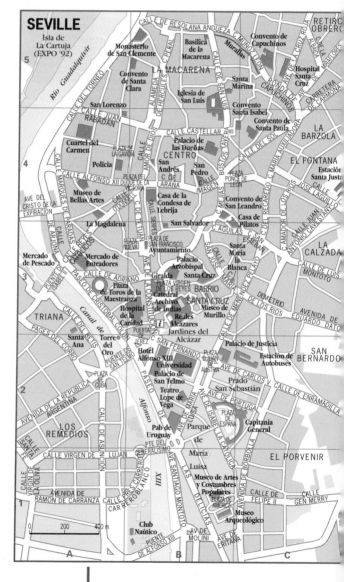

Seville

Seville is one of the most exciting cities in Europe. It is crammed with elegant shops, bars and restaurants, yet within the old quarter of the Barrio Santa Cruz lies a tangle of shaded alleyways, plazas and patios of almost village-like character. The great monuments of the cathedral, the Giralda and the Reales Alcázares apart, Seville has numerous other superb attractions. The vibrant cultural and social world of the city spills over into almost every aspect of life, mixing the very best of the past with modern elegance and fashion.

Seville generates style and romance like heat from the sun. Think Carmen and Don Juan and you have some measure of the city's passionate, if sometimes theatrical character. Yet there is an easy-going element about Seville that is essentially of the Mediterranean.

The city evolved as a historic trading centre for the gold and silver of the Sierra Morena. It was controlled by the Romans and then by the Moors from 712 until the Christian conquest of 1258. The discovery of the Americas made Seville one of the greatest ports and cities in Europe. Decline came with the silting of the Guadalquivir, but the glory of Seville has lasted into modern times.

Seville's main focus is its magnificent cathedral and Giralda tower (➤ 81) and adjacent Alcázar (➤ 24). South of the cathedral, beyond the Avenida de la Constitución, is the commercial district. Northeast of the cathedral is the delightful old Jewish quarter of Barrio Santa Cruz, while a little farther north is one of Sevilla's hidden gems, the 16th-century mansion, La Casa de Pilatos. Southeast of the cathedral are the public spaces of Plaza de España and the Maria Luisa Park. To the north lie the bustling Plaza de San Francisco and the great canopied shopping street of Calle Sierpes and its neighbours.

🚩 78B3
ℹ️ Avda. de la Constitución 21 ☎ 954 22 14 04; www.turismosevilla.org

Above: bustling traffic on the tree-lined Avenida de la Constitución

Below: the Patio de los Naranjos, the 'Courtyard of the Orange Trees' a serene relic of Seville's mosque now incorporated into the Cathedral

What to See in Seville

BARRIO SANTA CRUZ ✪✪✪

A first experience of the tightly–knit alleyways of the Barrio Santa Cruz can seem claustrophobic. Tall buildings shut out the sun; their stonework is dark and gloomy; the mood seems more northern European than Andalucían. But the Barrio eventually captivates. Santa Cruz was the *aljama*, or Jewish quarter, of the medieval city and was greatly changed after the Jewish community was expelled in 1492. The area was much restored and refurbished in the first years of the 20th century, and its narrow, muffled streets are a wonderful antidote to the raging traffic of Seville's busy main thoroughfares. Wander at will or follow a plan (➤ 83) and soon you will discover flower–filled corners such as Plaza Santa Cruz, the Jardines de Murillo on the Barrio's eastern boundary, and the Plaza Doña Elvira. There are numerous bars and cafés in which to take a break along the way.

LA CASA DE PILATOS ✪✪✪

The Casa de Pilatos (Pilatos House) is one of Seville's finest treasures. Built in 1519 the house was said to be a copy of Pontius Pilate's house in Jerusalem, but there is no real evidence confirming this. The entire building is a glorious celebration of the Mudéjar style mixed with the most elegant of Italianate features. To have such sustained Mudéjar design in one building is a delight. The *azulejos* tiling is outstanding; the patios, arcades, stairways and richly furnished salons are all superb. As an experience, this is the best place to truly get a feel for the subtle complexities of this unique architecture. There is hardly a finer self–contained complex of late medieval style and design in all of Andalucía.

✚ 78B3
✉ East of cathedral
🍴 Great mix of bars, cafés and restaurants (€–€€€)
♿ Few

Above: *the exquisite Patio Principal at the heart of the Casa de Pilatos*

Right: *the Giralda, named after the 'giraldillo', the 16th-century weather vane that surmounts it*

✚ 78C3
✉ Plaza Pilatos 1
☎ 954 22 52 98
🕐 Daily 9–6
🍴 Bodega Extraména, c/ San Esteban (€€)
🚌 C1, C2, C3, C4 (for Plaza San Augustín)
♿ Few
💰 Expensive

LA CATEDRAL Y LA GIRALDA ✪✪

Seville's cathedral and its adjoining Giralda tower are among some of the most visited monuments in Europe. At busy times, the weight of people seems to diminish the grandeur of it all, and, in the Giralda, especially, the climbing of the tower's 34 ramps and 17 final steps becomes something of a weary trudge. Brace yourself for a shrieking stream of downward–hurtling youngsters, not surprisingly letting off steam after a heavy day of organised 'culture'. Yet these are stunning buildings by any measure. The cathedral is said to be the largest Gothic church in the world. It replaced a Muslim mosque, and was a gesture of unashamed Christian triumphalism. The cavernous interior seems almost too vast to express anything other than empty pride, but the magnificent altarpiece in the sanctuary, intense focus of countless guided groups, is breathtaking in its exuberant design, and the choir and Renaissance Royal Chapel are just as striking. Outstanding works of art and religious artefacts fill the cathedral, and the alleged tomb of Christopher Columbus makes an eyecatching theatrical piece.

You can achieve momentary fitness, or exhaustion, by climbing the Giralda, the surviving 12th-century minaret of the original mosque, a structure that was heightened in 1565 by the addition of a bell tower and crowned by a bronze weather vane (*giraldillo*). The tower's exterior is its true glory, but the views from its upper gallery are impressive, and extend as far as distant olive groves to the northwest.

Sidebar:
- 78B3
- ✉ Plaza Virgen de los Reyes
- ☎ 954 21 49 71
- 🕐 Mon–Sat 11–5, Sun 2:30–6
- 🍴 Numerous bars, cafés and restaurants in C/ Mateos Gago (€–€€€)
- 🚌 Avenida de la Constitución
- ♿ Few
- Moderate; free Sun

MUSEO DE BELLAS ARTES ✪✪

The Museo de Bellas Artes (Fine Arts Museum) is one of Spain's major art galleries. Located in a beautiful old convent, La Merced Calzada, it contains 14 rooms displaying superb painting and sculpture. Highlights are works by Zurbarán and Murillo, including the latter's *Virgin and Child*, the famous 'La Servilleta', so named because the 'canvas' is said to be a dinner napkin. There are other works by Goya, Velázquez and El Greco. Room 5, once the convent church, is a dazzling place; its painted roof and Murillo collection are unforgettable.

Sidebar:
- 78A4
- ✉ Plaza del Museo 9
- ☎ 954 22 18 29
- 🕐 Tue 3–8, Wed–Sat 9–8, Sun 9–2
- 🍴 El Patio, San Eloy 9 (€–€€)
- 🚌 C1, C2, C3, C4
- ♿ Few
- Cheap; free with EU passport

PLAZA DE ESPAÑA AND MARÍA LUISA PARK ✪✪

Seville's remarkable Plaza de España and the María Luisa Park were the crowning glories of the city's ill–fated 1929 Ibero-American Exhibition, a grandiose event that failed to measure up to expectations. The Plaza and park are, however, great legacies. The Plaza is a huge semicircular complex of buildings lined with colourful motifs in *azulejos* tiling and fronted by a short length of canal, spanned by ornamental bridges. The Maria Luísa Park is a glorious stretch of wooded gardens, drenched in flowering plants. Beyond are the Museo Arqueológico (Archaeological Museum) and the Museo de Costumbres Populares (Popular Arts Museum), both fascinating.

🚺 78B2
✉ Avda de Isabel la Católica
🕐 Tue 3– 8, Wed–Sat 9–8, Sun 9–2
🍴 La Raza, Isabel la Católica 2 (€–€€)
🚌 C1, C2, C3, C4
♿ Good
🎟 Free

The Plaza de España is a flamboyant expression of Spain before the Civil War

ITÁLICA ✪

The Roman ruins of Itálica lie 9km north of Seville and can be reached by regular bus from the city's Plaza de Arma bus station. Itálica is remarkable, not least for its amphitheatre and for the ruins of its Roman city.

🚺 28B3
✉ Santiponce
☎ 955 99 73 76
🕐 Closed Mondays and festivals
🖐 Cheap; free with EU passport

REALES ALCÁZARES (➤ 24,TOP TEN)

A Walk Through the Barrio Santa Cruz

This is a basic tour of the Barrio's old Jewish quarter; you can divert at will down numerous alleyways on the way.

From Plaza Virgen de los Reyes walk up c/ Mateos Gago and at the junction go right down Mesón del Moro. At the junction with Ximenez de Encisco go left, then right down Cruces to a small square.

At the centre of the square are three slightly incongruous columns, the most conspicuous survivors of Roman Seville.

Leave the square by its left–hand corner and go down Mariscal into Plaza de Refinadores. (You can divert into the pleasant Jardines de Murillo here.) Go right, across the back of the Plaza, then down Mezquita into Plaza de Santa Cruz.

Just off Plaza de Santa Cruz is c/ Santa Teresa. The Museo de Murillo at No 8 traces the life of painter Bartolomé Esteban Murillo (1617–82), who lived there.

Leave Plaza de Santa Cruz by its left–hand corner and enter Plaza Alfaro. Go right along Lope de Rueda, then right to reach Reinosa. Go left, then left again at Jamerdana to Plaza de los Venerables.

There are guided tours (daily 10–2, 4–8) of the Hospicio de los Venerables Sacerdotes, which has a marvellous patio and superb paintings.

Leave the Plaza along Gloria lane to reach the Plaza Doña Elvira. Leave by the Vida and go into Judería. Turn right, then go through vaulted archways to Patio de Banderas. Cross the square and go under the archway to Plaza del Triunfo and the cathedral.

Distance
1.5km

Time
About 3 hours, with visits to museums

Start/End point
Plaza Virgen de los Reyes
✚ 78B3

Lunch
Hostería del Laurel (€€)
✉ Plaza de los Venerables 5
☎ 954 22 02 95

Plaza Doña Elvira, a green oasis at the heart of the Barrio Santa Cruz

The ancient arches of Aracena's 13th-century church, Nuestra Señora de los Dolores

What to See in Seville & Huelva

ARACENA

Aracena's most lauded attraction is the limestone cave complex, the Gruta de las Maravillas (Grotto of Marvels, ► 19). But Aracena and its surroundings have much to offer above ground. The town surrounds a hilltop medieval castle ruin and its adjacent church of Nuestra Señora de los Dolores; there are pleasant bars and cafés in the surrounding streets.

About 20km south of Aracena along the scenic A479 is Minas de Río Tinto and the desolate yet compelling landscape of the area's open-cast mines, where copper, silver, and iron have been mined for thousands of years. The **Mining Museum**, on a hill above the village of Río Tinto, is excellent.

AROCHE

The charming hilltop village of Aroche lies only 24km from the border with Portugal. Its Moorish castle, originally established in the 9thcentury, was rebuilt substantially in 1923 and now incorporates one of Andalucía's most eccentric bullrings, as well as the village's archaeological museum. Ask for permission to obtain access at the Town Hall if the castle is closed. Just below the castle is the peaceful church of Nuestra Señora de la Asunción. The village has another grand eccentricity which is worth looking at in the Museo del Santo Rosario (Museum of Rosaries) in c/Alférez Carlos Lobos. Aroche's main square, Plaza de España, has a good number of café-bars and is a delightful place to while away a few hours, watching the world go by.

28B3
89km northwest of Seville
Several (€–€€)
Daily from Seville and Huelva

Río Tinto Mining Museum
28B3
Plaza del Museo
959 59 00 25/59 10 65
Tue, Thu, Sat, Sun 10–2, Wed 5–8
Cheap

28A3
33km west of Aracena
Bars and cafés in main square (€)
Daily, Aracena–Aroche
None
Holy Week. Pilgrimage of San Mamés , Whitsun. Feria de Agosto, Aug. Pilgrimage, Jun

---

CARMONA ✪✪

Carmona stands on a high escarpment overlooking the fertile valleys of the Río Corbones and the Río Guadalquivir. Over 4km of ancient walls enclose old Carmona, and the main entrances to the town are through magnificent Roman gateways, the Puerta de Sevilla and the Puerta de Córdoba The lively and sun-drenched Plaza de San Fernando, circular and fringed by trees, has some eye-catching buildings, and near by is the spacious market, a big patio enclosed by arcades.

Follow the narrow c/ Martín López de Córdoba out of Plaza de San Fernando to reach the church of Santa María la Mayor. The church is entered through the delightful Patio de los Naranjos, the entrance patio of the mosque that originally stood here, still with its orange trees and horseshoe arches. The church has a soaring Gothic nave and powerful *retablo*. Uphill, c/ G Freire leads to Carmona's superbly located Alcazar del Rey de Pedro, now an exclusive *parador*.

The Seville Gate incorporates the Moorish Alcazar de Abajo, where Carmona's helpful tourism office is located. Beyond the gate, across the busy Plaza Blas Infante, is modern Carmona, dominated by the handsome church of San Pedro, whose great tower replicates the style of Seville's Giralda and which has a wonderful baroque sacristy. A wide and busy promenade leads to Carmona's **Roman Necropolis**, a beautifully preserved series of dramatic burial chambers and one of the most remarkable archaeological sites in Andalucía.

✚ 28B3
✉ 30km west of Aracena
ℹ Arco de la Puerta de Sevilla ☎ 954 19 09 55
🍴 Several bars, cafés and restaurants (€–€€)
🚌 Daily, Seville–Carmona
♿ Few
❓ Carnival, Feb. Holy Week

Roman Necropolis
✉ Avda de Jorge Bonsor 9
☎ 954 14 08 11
🕐 Mid-Jun–mid-Sep Tue–Sat 9–2, Sun 10–2; Mid-Sep–mid-Jun Tue–Fri 9–5, Sat and Sun 10–2
♿ Few

The handsome tower of the church of Santa María la Mayor seen from Carmona's central Plaza de San Fernando

Food & Drink

Andalucían cuisine reflects the distinctive spirit and ambience of southern Spain through its use of local produce from land and sea, through the needs and tastes of its rural communities and through lingering elements of Moorish cooking. Fish is a popular feature of Andalucían cuisine and fresh vegetables enhance traditional meat dishes, while the cured ham of the Andalucían mountains is renowned. Fresh fruit is also available in abundance. Complementing all of this are the fortified wines: the famous *generosos*, the sherries of southwest Andalucía.

Fish (*Pescados*)

Almería, Málaga, Huelva and numerous coastal villages are noted for their *fritura* (fried fish), but for quality and quantity of fish dishes, Cádiz, Sanlúcar de Barrameda and Jerez de la Frontera are the top spots. Here, fried fish platters of small flat fish and red mullet are a standard favourite, as is *arroz marinera*, a fish-based *paella*. On the beaches of the Costa del Sol and in Málaga, look out for *chiringuitos*, beach-front bars that specialise in fried or grilled *boquerones* (anchovies), *sardinas* (sardines) and *chanquetes* (whitebait). In more sophisticated restaurants the choice of fish dishes is huge, many based on *atún* (tuna fish), *pez espada* (swordfish) and shellfish such as lobster and prawns.

Above:
classic shellfish paella
Below: *succulent cured hams, the* jamon serrano *of Las Alpujarras*

Beef & Pork (*Carne*)

The meat stew of Andalucía, the *cocido*, is a standard favourite but one that varies greatly in its ingredients from region to region. Another classic dish is *cola*, or *rabo de toro guisado* (bull's tail stew), a favourite after bullfights but often advertised as oxtail stew. The mountain regions of the Sierra Nevada and Sierra Morena produce the finest cured ham. The *jamón serrano* (mountain ham) of Trevélez in Las Alpujarras, produced from white pigs, is a great favourite, as is the *pata negra* of the Jabugo and Aracena region of the western Sierra Morena, produced from acorn–fed black pigs. Other pork products include *chorizo* (spicy sausage), *salchichón* (salami) and *morcilla* (blood sausage).

Fresh fruit and vegetables are plentiful and varied in Andalucían markets

Gazpacho

The most famous Andalucían dish is *gazpacho*, a soup that originated as a field-workers' meal and comprised a bread and garlic paste, salted and mixed with olive oil and hot water and drunk throughout the working day. The soup leftover had vinegar and water added and was drunk cold. *Gazpacho* evolved with the addition of tomatoes, peppers and cucumber, and today there are numerous variations to this excellent starter to a restaurant meal.

Desserts (Postres)

Meals in Andalucía are often rounded off with fresh fruit, rather than elaborate desserts. *Helado* (ice cream) is often available, however, and other sweets include cream-filled pastries and crème caramel. For the sweet of tooth, however, the famous Andalucían *dulces*, mouthwatering sweet cakes, a lingering legacy of Moorish times, are available in *pastelerías* (cake shops) and in various convents, which produce some exquisite regional specialities.

Cheese & Eggs (*Queso & Huevos*)

Andalucían cheese is usually produced from goat's milk and sometimes sheep's milk, but rarely from cow's milk. Cheeses can be very local and have distinctive local flavours that can be quite strong. Fine cheeses are produced in Aracena and Grazalema and also in Las Alpujarras and in Ronda. Eggs play an important part in *tapas* making and form the basis of the famous *tortilla* (potato-based omelette).

Wine (*Vino*)

Red wine (*tinto*) is the best wine to look for in Andalucía, but is often imported from other parts of Spain, Valdepeñas and Rioja being familiar names to most visitors. There are locally produced red and white wines, and the red wines of Las Alpujarras and other rural areas can be very good. Refreshing drinks are *tinto de verano*, a mix of red wine with ice, and *gaseosa*, a type of lemonade.

Sherry is, of course, the great drink of Andalucía: white wine fortified with alcohol, and subtly refined. Classic sherry comes in the form of *fino* (dry), *amontillado* (medium) and *oloroso* (full–bodied and slightly sweet); *fino* is the ultimate, chilled accompaniment to *tapas*. Other splendid sherry-like wines, not fortified with alcohol, are *montilla* from Córdoba province and *manzanillas* from the Sanlúcar de Barrameda area.

Brandy is also produced by the sherry *bodegas*. Andalucía is Spain's major producer of brandy and is thus a connoisseur's delight. The great morning pick-me-up is *anís*, a sweet or dry aniseed–based drink.

White wine of Cádiz

A Drive Through the Sierra Norte

Distance
220km

Time
Eight hours, with stops

Start/End point
Carmona
✚ 28B3

Lunch
Restaurante del Moro (€)
✉ C/ Paseo El Moro,
Carmona
☎ 954 88 43 26

This drive takes you through the lesser-known parts of Seville province: the remote Parque Natural de la Sierra Norte.

Leave Carmona by the Seville Gate and follow signs for Lora del Río on the A457. After 20km, go left at a junction. Cross the Río Guadalquivir and the railway line, then go left on the A431 to a junction before Alcalá del Río. Take the first exit (signed C433 Burguillos and Castilblanco). Stay on the C433 to Castilblanco, then follow signs for Cazalla de la Sierra on the C433.

You are now entering the Parque Natural de la Sierra Norte. The road winds through lonely hills swathed in cork oak, holm oak, pine and chestnut. Vulture, eagle and black stork are found here and deer, wild boar, wild cat and mountain goat haunt the woodlands and rocky tops.

At a junction with the A432 go left (signed El Pedroso). At El Pedroso go right at a roundabout (signed A432 Constantina, Cazalla de la Sierra). Cross the railway and follow signs to Cazalla.

The impressive Puerto de Sevilla, the 'Seville Gate', guards the southern entrance to Carmona

Cazalla de la Sierra is a pleasant country town, famous for its cherry brandy.

Leave Cazalla from its northern end, following signs for Constantina on the A455. Drive through wooded countryside, cross the railway at the isolated Constantina station and continue to Constantina.

Constantina is dominated by the medieval Castillo de la Armada, on a high hill, and has a charming old quarter.

Continue south from Constantina on the A455 to Lora del Río. Re-cross the railway line, then retrace your route back to Carmona.

*Écija's 15th-century
Church of Santiago has
outstanding Renaissance
and Mudéjar façades*

ÉCIJA ★★

This Ciudad de las Torres, (City of Towers) is all dramatic skyline. Eleven magnificent church towers, steepled, domed, and exquisitely decorated with colourful tiles, punctuate the sky, each with its resident storks. The town is much more than its towers, of course, There are remarkable 18th-century façades, so fluid in their forms that they hint at the work of Barcelona's Antoní Gaudí. Track down the Palacio de Peñaflor in c/Castellar. It is a remarkable building, painted and sinuous and with a flamboyant baroque portal, lacking only a wider street to set if off. The Palacio de Benameji in c/ Cánovas del Castillo, home to the tourist office and a town museum, is another delight. Écija's splendid central square the Plaza Mayor, or Plaza de España has been walled off for the construction of an underground car park, which has robbed the encircling arcades and pleasant cafés of light and air; all the more reason to admire the glorious church towers.

✚ 28C3
✉ 80km east of Seville
🍴 Several bars, cafés and
restaurants (€–€€)
▣ Daily, Seville-Écija
ℹ c/ de Cánovas del Castillo
4 ☎ 955 90 29 33
♿ Few
❓ Holy Week. Feria de
Primavera (Spring Fair),
8 May
☎ 955 90 29 33

HUELVA ★

Huelva is the fourth largest port in Spain. The city has paid a price for centuries of industry and commerce, and displays a grim approach from any direction. Yet its heart has great charm and life. The palm–fringed main square, Plaza de las Monjas, is surrounded by busy streets. A short distance east along the arcaded Avda Martín Alonso Pinzón, in Alameda Sundheim, is Huelva's impressive Museo Provincial. Northeast is the curious Barrio Reina Victoria, or the Barrio Inglés, an Anglicised complex of housing, a legacy of the Rio Tinto company.

✚ 28A3
✉ 90km west of Seville
ℹ Avenida de Alemania 12
☎ 959 25 74 03
🚂 Estación de Ferrocarril,
Avda de Italia
☎ 902 24 02 02
🚌 Estación de Autobuses,
Avda de Portugal 9
☎ 959 25 69 00
♿ Few

28A3
✉ 15km east of Huelva
ℹ Castillo s/n
☎ 959 37 18 98
🚌 Daily, Huelva–Moguer
♿ Few
❓ Romería de Montemayor, Sun, 2nd May. Corpus Christi

MOGUER ●●

Moguer is one of the smartest and friendliest towns in Andalucía. The pretty central square, Plaza Cabildo, has a superb neo-classical Town Hall, framed by palm trees. Opposite, in a little square, there is a bronze bust of Juan Ramón Jiménez, a native son and a Nobel Prize-winning poet (▶ 14). There is a Jiménez c/ Juan Ramón Museum at c/ Jiménez 5, the writer's birthplace. In nearby Plaza de las Monjas, the 14th-century Convento Santa Clara is now a museum and art gallery, with a Mudéjar-style cloister and delightful church The church is still used for worship. Adjoining it is the equally splendid Convento de San Francisco.

DID YOU KNOW?

Moguer has strong connections with Christopher Columbus. The town contributed the caravel La Niña, one of the three ships that made first landfall in America, and her captain and navigator, Juan and Pedro Alonso Niño came from the town along with many of Columbus's crewmen. Columbus is also said to have visited the Convent for an all night prayer vigil in thanksgiving for his safe return from his first voyage.

28C3
✉ 80km east of Seville
🍴 Large selection of bars, cafés and restaurants (€–€€)
🚌 Daily, Seville–Osuna, Granada–Osuna, Malaga–Osuna
♿ Few
❓ Holy Week. Feria, 13–15 May. Pilgrimage of La Virgen de la Consolación, 8 Sep

The Convento Santa Clara in the Plaza de las Monjas

OSUNA ●

Osuna's long main street, Carrera Caballos, narrow and constrained and meant for more stately traffic, reverberates with a constant stream of cars and motorbikes. Away from the main street, old Osuna preserves its noble past with a host of dignified mansions and stunning Renaissance façades. High above the lower town stand the monumental buildings of the old university and the magnificent Renaissance Colegiata church, with its gilded retablo, airy interior hung with fine paintings and atmospheric crypt. Just down from the Colegiata is the convent of La Encarnación, with beautiful *azulejos* tiling. The main square of Osuna, the Plaza Mayor, is a rather gloomy space, but Carrera Caballos, though traffic-bound, is a lively, long street full of shops, bars and restaurants.

Where To...

Above: a flower seller in Seville's busy
Calle Sierpes
Right: a bullfight poster

Córdoba and Jaén

Prices
Prices are approximate, based on a meal for one including wine and service
€ = up to €18
€€ = €18–€35
€€€ = over €35

Tapas
The *tapa* takes the form of a snack or titbit that can range from a few olives or a sliver of *jamón serrano* (dried ham) on oil-soaked bread to more elaborate mixtures of fish, meat, cheese and vegetables. The word *tapa* means 'lid' and the *tapa* tradition may have derived from the habit of covering drinks with a small dish or a slice of bread to protect them from insects and dust. The *tapeo*, an evening jaunt round the bars enjoying *tapas*, ideally accompanied by chilled *fino* sherry or beer, (never by coffee), is now enshrined in the food lore of Andalucía.

Córdoba
El Caballo Rojo (€€€)
Excellent Córdoban cuisine at this famous restaurant near the Mezquita, frequented by royalty when they're in town. Specialises in classic local dishes, such as partridge breasts, lamb and honey and *rabo de toro* (oxtail).
⊠ Cardenal Herrero 28
☎ 957 47 53 75
🕐 Lunch and dinner

Los Califas (€€)
Attractive restaurant in the old quarter and with a pleasant rooftop terrace. Specialises in Córdoban regional cuisine, with good meat specialities.
⊠ c/ Deanes 3 ☎ 957 47 13 20 🕐 Lunch and dinner

El Churrasco (€€)
Top quality restaurant whose staff and management are rather well aware of the fact. Andalucían cuisine at its finest, with dishes such as *gaspacho de habas*, delicious cold soup made from broad beans and spiced with almonds and other delicacies. Top end of price range for special dishes, but with reasonable set menu otherwise.
⊠ Calle Romero 16
☎ 957 29 08 19 🕐 Lunch and dinner. Closed Aug

Pizzaiolo (€)
Well-run pizzeria in attractive square. Good selection of tasty, if predictable food. Features, proudly, in *Guinness Book of Records* as having 360 different selections.
⊠ CalleSan Felipe 5
☎ 957 48 64 33
🕐 Lunch and dinner

Taberna San Miguel (€)
One of Córdoba's most popular establishments, with a lively ambience and a wide selection of tapas.
⊠ Plaza San Miguel 1
☎ 957 47 83 28
🕐 Lunch and dinner

Baeza
Casa Juanito (€€)
Tasty and unusual dishes based on traditional recipes. Specialities include partridge salad, fillet of beef with tomatoes and peppers and artichoke hearts with tomatoes and garlic. In the hotel of the same name.
⊠ Avenida Arca del Agua
☎ 953 74 00 40 🕐 Lunch and dinner. Closed dinner Sun and Mon

La Góndola (€)
Cosy local bar and restaurant with brick and tile interior and open fireplace. *Tapas* include the tasty speciality, *patatas baezanas*, sautéed potatoes topped with fried mushrooms, parsley and garlic.
⊠ Portales Carboneria 13
☎ 953 74 29 84 🕐 Lunch and dinner

Cazorla
Juan Carlos (€–€€)
Popular restaurant in the centre of town serving a wide choice of interesting game dishes, as well as some innovative starters, such as cream of melon soup with mint. Excellent desserts, including home-made fig ice-cream.
⊠ Plaza Consuela Mendieta 2
☎ 953 72 12 01 🕐 Lunch and dinner

Parador de Cazorla (€€€)
Making your way along

forested mountain roads to this quality restaurant, part of Cazorla's *parador*, is a fine preparation for good Sierra cuisine including *gachamiga*, a tasty bacon dish. Reservations advised for non-residents.

✉ **Sierra Cazorla s/n**
☎ **953 72 70 75** 🕐 **Dinner**

Jaén

Casa Vicente (€€€)

Top Jaén eating place, housed in a restored palace near the cathedral. Excellent local cuisine with game specialities.

✉ **Calle Francisco Marín Mora 1** ☎ **953 22 22 22** 🕐 **Lunch and dinner. Closed Sun dinner and Aug**

Parador de Jaén (€€)

High-quality cuisine in high surroundings at the restaurant of Jaén's Moorish *parador*. Andalucían specialities such as the famous *morcilla en caldera* (blood sausage), served in mock-medieval surroundings. Reservations advised for non-residents.

✉ **Castillo de Santa Catalina**
☎ **953 23 00 00** 🕐 **Dinner**

Priego de Córdoba

El Alijibe (€–€€)

Friendly tapas bar and restaurant opposite the stunning Iglesia de la Asunción, serving unusual local dishes such as dates stuffed with bacon. More formal restaurant downstairs with a reasonably priced *menu del día*.

✉ **Calle Abad Palomino 7**
☎ **957 70 18 56**

Rafi (€)

Part of the Hostal Rafi, this relaxed restaurant has tasty local dishes served in a cheerful atmosphere and often in the company of friendly locals.

✉ **c/ Isabel la Catolica 4**
☎ **957 54 07 49**
🕐 **Lunch and dinner**

Segura de la Sierra

Bar Peralta (€)

Located on the way up to the entrance arch to the upper town, this local bar serves *tapas* and *raciones* and does tasty plate-loads of pork crackling.

✉ **c/ Regidor Juan de Isla 12**
☎ **953 48 00 13**
🕐 **Lunch and evening meal**

Úbeda

El Gallo Rojo (€)

Good value at this popular restaurant to the north of Plaza de Andalucía. Regional dishes can be enjoyed at outside tables, a reasonable distance from a busy junction. Reservations advised.

✉ **Calle Manuel Barraca 3**
☎ **953 75 20 38** 🕐 **Lunch and dinner**

El Marqués (€€)

Pleasant restaurant where the terrace has a view to the 16th-century Palacio de la Rambla. Reasonably priced regional dishes in fine surroundings.

✉ **Plaza del Marqués de la Rambla s/n** ☎ **953 75 72 55**
🕐 **Lunch and dinner**

Meson Barbacoa (€)

Intriguing restaurant-cum-agricultural museum. The walls are crammed with farming implements and the rafters hung with traditional bags, baskets and containers. Good selection of *platos combinados* to go with it.

✉ **c/ San Cristobal 17** ☎ **953 79 04 73** 🕐 **Lunch and dinner**

Zuheros

Restaurant Zuhayra (€€)

Located in the hotel of the same name and with a good selection of local dishes, often flavoured with the area's famous olive oil. Córdoba province's equally famous *montilla* wine should be compulsory.

✉ **c/ Mirador 10** ☎ **957 69 46 93** 🕐 **Lunch and dinner**

Pincho, Ración and Plato Combinado

The smallest *tapa* is often referred to as a *pincho*. More substantial helpings of *tapas* are called *raciónes* and are a meal in themselves. A *ración* should cost no more than about €6. A popular option is a *plato combinado*, a mix of food with bread and often a drink. A *plato combinado* should cost no more than about €8. Pictures of the choice of *platos combinados* available at each restaurant are often displayed.

Tapas Tip

Most *tapas* that include tuna fish, *atún*, are fairly certain to be tasty. Try *redondillos de atún*, if you come across it. This is tuna mixed with eggs and breadcrumbs cooked in a white wine sauce .

Granada and Almería

Table Charges

In city bars and cafés there are varying charges for the same *tapas* or *raciónes*, depending on where you eat. Standing at the bar in time-honoured *tapeo* fashion will cost the least. Eating at a table will cost more and eating outside on the pavement or 'terrace' may cost more again. If you eat at the bar, pay at the bar. If you want to sit at a table, whether inside or outside, expect waiter service.

Tapas Tip

You can make a complete meal out of *tapas* by selecting several different dishes between two and sharing them out. Many Andalucíans make selective *tapas*-eating their main intake for the evening. It also discourages drink from going to your head.

Alhama de la Granada
Meson Diego (€)

Good local café-restaurant where you may even enjoy free *tapas* with your drinks before ordering a sit-down meal at the broad terrace, usually in the company of local people, alongside Alhama's pleasant central square.

✉ **Plaza Constitucion 12**
☎ **958 36 01 21**
🕐 **Lunch and dinner**

Almeria
El Bello Rincón (€€)

Considered to be one of Almería's top restaurants, offering wonderful sea views and excellent fresh seafood.

✉ **Ctra. Nacional 340 Km 436**
☎ **950 23 84 27**
🕐 **Lunch and dinner. Closed Mon, Jul and Aug**

Bodega Las Botas (€€)

Well aware of its appeal, this delightful *tapas* bar is still irresistible. Try and sit at the barrel tables if you're sampling wine – and there's plenty of choice – or at the neat little tables on the other side of the bar for *jámon* and fish dishes at their best.

✉ **c/Fructuoso Pérez 3**
🕐 **Dinner**

Asador Torreluz (€€)

Part of the Torreluz Hotel complex located on Almería's charming Plaza Flores this top-class restaurant is renowned for its local and international cuisine.

✉ **Plaza Flores 1** ☎ **950 23 43 99** 🕐 **Lunch and dinner**

Bubión
La Artesa Restaurante (€€)

Attractive small bar and restaurant specialising in roast leg of pork and *choto al ajillo* (kid cooked with garlic). The dark wood and bright tilework is typically Andalucian.

✉ **Carretera de la Sierra 2**
☎ **958 76 34 37** 🕐 **Lunch and dinner. Closed Mon**

Capileira
Poqueira (€)

Good little restaurant attached to the hotel of the same name. Local dishes at their best and from a reasonably priced menu.

✉ **C/ Doctor Castilla 6**
☎ **958 76 30 48**
🕐 **Lunch and dinner**

Granada
Chikito (€€)

Popular 'literary' eating place once patronised by García Lorca and his contemporaries and by English writers on the romantic Andalucían trail. Just north of the Carrera del Genil promenade in a leafy square. Expensive international dishes, but with a reasonably priced (for Granada) set menu.

✉ **Plaza del Campillo 9**
☎ **958 22 33 64**
🕐 **Lunch and dinner**

Cunini (€)

Popular establishment with a lively atmosphere and a good reputation for its seafood.

✉ **Plaza Pescadería 14**
☎ **958 25 07 77**
🕐 **Lunch and dinner. Closed dinner Sun and Mon**

Mirador de Morayma (€€)

Housed in a handsome 16th-century mansion in the old quarter of Albaicín, this restaurant has good cuisine. The delightful leafy terrace has magnificent views over

the Alhambra
✉ **Pianista Garcia Carillo 2, Albaicín** ☎ 958 22 82 90
🕐 **Lunch and dinner. Closed Sun**

Sevilla (€€)
This venerable Granadine restaurant located at the heart of the cathedral area offers a reasonably priced menu. There's also a good *tapas* bar, and a pleasant outside seating area.
✉ **Officios 12** ☎ **958 22 12 23**
🕐 **Lunch and dinner. Closed Sun evenings**

San Nicolás (€€€)
A strikingly elegant restaurant with columns and chandeliers. Choose a table by the window for breathtaking views of the Alhambra. The menu includes such nouvelle-Andaluz dishes as leg of pork filled with lavender and honey.
✉ **Calle San Nicolás 3**
☎ **958 80 42 862**
🕐 **Lunch and dinner. Closed Sun, Tue lunch**

Guadix
Comercio (€€)
This top-quality restaurant is located in the hotel of the same name. It has won several prestigious awards for its cooking, so the local and international specialities on offer come highly recommended.
✉ **c/ Mira de Amezcua 3**
☎ **958 66 05 00**
🕐 **Lunch and dinner**

Mojacar
El Homo (€€)
Elegant restaurant in the charming Hostal Mamabel's, with a good reputation for the quality of the cuisine.

✉ **Calle Embajadores 5**
☎ **950 47 24 48** 🕐 **Lunch and dinner**

Parador de Mojácar (€€€)
Fine selection of local cuisine in this attractive modern restaurant, part of the Mojácar *parador*. Try *gambones de Gaurruchera*, a tasty prawn dish. Delicious desserts, also. Reservations advised for non-residents.
✉ **Playa de Mojácar s/n**
☎ **950 47 82 50** 🕐 **Dinner**

Trevélez
Meson La Fragua (€)
Located in hotel of the same name. Good substantial local dishes with *jámon serrano* to the fore.
✉ **c/ San Antonio 4** ☎ **958 85 86 26; fax 958 85 86 14**
🕐 **Lunch and dinner**

Velez Blanco
Bar Sociedad (€)
Classic village bar/café where you can sample *tapas* and *raciónes* in the company of friendly locals and watch the world go by on the small roadside terrace.
✉ **c/ Corredera s/n**
☎ **950 41 50 27**
🕐 **Breakfast, lunch, dinner**

Mesón El Molino (€€)
A relaxed eating place tucked away in a narrow alley just off the village's main street. A good range of regional dishes in pleasant and relaxing surroundings.
✉ **Plaza Curtidores 1**
☎ **950 41 50 70**
🕐 **Dinner. Closed during winter months**

Breakfast
Breakfast (*desayuno*) can be had at local bars and cafés by 8AM and even earlier, but for most visitors breakfast at about 10AM is usual and is at its most enjoyable when taken on a café terrace, in the shade. Orange juice is the genuine article, and is delicious. You can follow this with *tostadas*, big slices of roll which can be doused with olive oil from metal jugs or spread with butter and then jam (*mermelada*). Coffee is always available, but if you want tea, do not ask for tea with milk (*té con leche*). Make it clear that you want the tea black, and that milk should be brought to you separately; otherwise you might end up with a soggy tea bag drowning in boiled milk. *Chocolate y churros* (hot chocolate and spiral-shaped doughnuts) are another popular option for breakfast, especially during the winter months. There's really no such thing as a breakfast *tapas*, but if you want something other than *tostadas* and *mermelada*, try a slice of *tortilla española* (potato omelette) or *jámon serrano* and *huevo cocido* (cured ham and boiled egg).

Málaga & Cádiz

When to Eat

American and North European-style snack bars and fast food establishments are on the increase in all of Spain's larger towns and cities. The *bocadillo* (French roll with a filling of your choice) is a popular lunch bite, and you will always be able to get some form of food at any time of the day in most cafés in the larger cities and on the Costa del Sol. The Costa caters more for North European eating habits than rural towns and villages do. Among Andalucíans, the climate and the working day dictate sensible eating patterns. Lunch is usually after 2PM and is often the day's main meal. Evening eating begins at about 8PM with drinks and *tapas*, and with supper from about 9PM onwards.

Antequera

El Angelote (€€)

Centrally located across from the museum, this excellent restaurant serves fine local cuisine. Try the *setas* (oyster mushrooms) with garlic and rosemary, or wild partridge. The desserts are delicious and more varied than the ice-cream and flan norm.

✉ Calle Encarnación (corner Coso Viejo) ☎ 952 70 34 65 🕐 Lunch and dinner. Closed Mon

La Espuela (€€)

Located in the bullring complex, and specialising in meat dishes including *rabo de toro* (bull's-tail stew), and partridge with rice. Outside seating area for hot evenings.

✉ Plaza de Toros de Antequera s/n ☎ 952 84 46 62 🕐 Lunch and dinner

Arcos de la Frontera

El Convento (€€)

Pleasant restaurant of hotel of same name, at the heart of the old town. Outstanding traditional cuisine with game dishes a speciality. You pay less for the set menu, but this is still quite expensive.

✉ Calle Maldonado 2 ☎ 956 70 23 33 🕐 Lunch and dinner. Closed 17–22 Jan

Cádiz

Balandro (€)

A local favourite with a pleasant terrace as well as an inside dining.area Excellent Cádiz fish and seafood *tapas*, and *raciones*..

✉ Alameda Apodaca 22 ☎ 956 22 09 92 🕐 Lunch and dinner

El Faro (€€)

Rated as one of the best fish restaurants around. The *paella* is excellent, as are the great local dishes featuring bream, octopus and hake.

✉ c/ San Felix 15 ☎ 956 22 9916 🕐 Lunch and dinner

Mesón Cumbres Mayores (€–€€)

Good lively tapas bar and restaurant. A great variety of dishes include fish, seafood and barbecued meats.

✉ Calle Zorilla ☎ 956 21 32 70 🕐 Lunch and dinner

Gibraltar

La Bayuca (€€€)

One of the oldest restaurants on the Rock, well known for its Mediterranean specialities with an extensive menu and emphasis on seafood. Delicious desserts and swift, friendly service.

✉ 21 Turnbull Lane ☎ 956 77 51 19 🕐 Lunch and dinner. Closed Sun lunch and Tue

Jerez

Gaitán (€€)

A prize-winning restaurant that offers good value traditional and nouvelle cuisine, with fish dishes a speciality.

✉ c/ Gaitáan 3 ☎ 956 34 58 59 🕐 Lunch and dinner. Closed Sun dinner

Málaga

Bar Lo Güeno (€)

One of the best-known *tapas* bars in Málaga, with more than 75 varieties to choose from. The L-shaped bar is very cramped, but there are tables outside.Excellent range of Rioja wines.

✉ c/Marín Garcia 9 ☎ 952 22 21 80 🕐 Lunch and dinner. Closed Sun

La Cancela (€)
A local favourite, this small restaurant has outdoor seating as well as small dining rooms inside. Dishes are authentically local and include *ago blanc* (a thick *gazpacho*-type soup made from garlic, almonds and grapes).
✉ c/ Denis Belgrano 3
☎ 952 22 31 25 🕐 Lunch and dinner. Closed Wed evening

Casa Pedro (€–€€)
Long-established, family-run fish restaurant in El Palo. The dining-room overlooks the sea and the seafood is very fresh. If you don't mind the noise and bustle, come here for Sunday lunch, when Malagueño families traditionally dine out
✉ Quitapenas 121, El Palo
☎ 952 29 00 13 🕐 Lunch and dinner. Closed Mon

Marbella
Santiago (€€€)
Elegant restaurant with a good position on the seafront. Offers top quality fish and seafood along with an extensive wine list.
✉ Paseo Marítimo 5 ☎ 952 77 43 39 🕐 Lunch and dinner. Closed Nov

Medina Sidonia
Bar Cádiz (€)
Centrally located bar-restaurant with a traditional menu and a good selection of *tapas*.
✉ Plaza España 14 ☎ 956 41 02 50 🕐 Lunch and dinner

Nerja
Casa Luque (€€)
One of Nerja's best-known establishments, housed in an old Andalucian mansion. Cuisine is from the north of Spain. The attractive patio is open for outdoor dining in summer.
✉ Plaza Cavana 2 ☎ 952 52 10 04 🕐 Lunch and dinner

Ronda
Pedro Romero (€€)
Popular, award-winning restaurant; walls covered in bullfighting photographs. *Rabo de toro a la Rondeña*, Ronda-style bull's-tail stew, is a speciality; or try the grilled salmon.
✉ Virgen de la Paz 18 ☎ 952 87 11 10 🕐 Lunch and dinner

Restaurant Don Miguel (€€)
Restaurant in a hotel of the same name, with indoor eating and spacious terraces on several levels offering dramatic views of Ronda's gorge.
✉ Plaza de España 4 ☎ 952 87 77 22 🕐 Lunch and dinner

Sanlúcar de Barrameda
Casa Bigote (€€)
The standard of fish cuisine is high in Sanlúcar, so restaurants with good reputations are of a very high standard indeed, and El Bigote is one of the best.
✉ Bajo de Guía s/n ☎ 956 36 26 96 🕐 Lunch and dinner

Tarifa
Bar Morilla (€)
Pleasant *tapas* bar with outside seating, at the very heart of the town. Good selection of local dishes.
✉ c/ Sancho IV El Bravo s/n
☎ 956 68 17 57
🕐 Lunch and dinner

Torremolinos
Bodega Quitapenas (€)
Much favoured by locals and tourists for its reasonably priced tapas and seafood dishes, and its position on the steps leading down to the beach. Always a hive of activity.
✉ Calle Cuesta del Tajo 3
🕐 Lunch and dinner

Tapas Tip
Unless you are fluent in Spanish and don't mind what you eat, be careful about sticking a pin in a typical menu board outside a bar, café or restaurant. A *tapa* can be anything from *chicharrón* (pork scratchings), to *criadillas* (fried testicles of pig), so make sure you know what a *tapa* is describing. Good names to look for in lists of *tapas* are *calamares* (squid), *anchoas* (anchovies), *champiñones* (mushrooms), *chorizo* (spicy sausage) and *jamón serrano* (cured ham). Names that might give you pause, or challenge the adventurous, are *callos* or *menudo* (tripe), *burgajo* or *caracoles* (snails), *sesos* (brains) and the Granada speciality, *tortilla al sacromonte* (omelette made with lambs' testicles and brains).

Huelva and Seville

Top Restaurants

The top Andalucían restaurants can match any in Europe for the quality of their cuisine, and you will find international dishes on offer in the best city restaurants. The more formal restaurants often include *Restaurante* or *Mesón* in their titles. Regional dishes are also available, and there are chefs producing new and exciting cuisine with a regional bias. Andalucía, especially in places such as Málaga, Cádiz and Sanlúcar de Barrameda, is famous for its fish dishes. A mainly fish restaurant is called a *marisquería* and, although the very best of these are found on the coast, many inland restaurants offer excellent fish dishes.

Tapas Tip

Pimientos rellenos (stuffed peppers), make for excellent *tapas*, or a starter for a restaurant meal. They may be stuffed with a mix of meat, cheese and even fish, and seasoned with a selection of sauces.

Aracena
Casas (€€)
Well-run, prize-winning restaurant specialising in traditional Sierra Morena cuisine. Impressive wine list. Restaurant is on the way up to the Gruta de la Maravillas.

- ✉ Casas. Colmenitas 41
- ☎ 959 12 82 12
- 🕐 Lunch and dinner

Ayamonte
Parador de Ayamonte (€€€)
Superb restaurant within this magnificent parador with its sweeping views of the river. Try the regional seafood specialities such as *calamar relleno* (stuffed squid) and *raya en pimiento* (stingray with red pepper).

- ✉ El Castillito (Ayamonte)
- ☎ 959 32 07 00
- 🕐 Lunch and dinner

Carmona
Alcázar del Rey Don Pedro (€€€)
Restaurant in Carmona's handsome *parador* and open to non-residents. High quality cuisine comprising local specialities and international dishes. They include *cartuja de perdiz* (partridge with vegetables). The Carmona can get very busy so reservations are advised.

- ✉ Alcázar, s/n ☎ 954 14 10 10
- 🕐 Lunch and dinner

La Almazara de Carmona (€€)
Moorish décor in a pleasant restaurant on the eastern side of town. There is a good selection of salads and vegetable dishes using fresh local produce. The home-made desserts are particularly excellent.

- ✉ Santa Anna 33 ☎ 954 19 00 76 🕐 Lunch and dinner

Meson La Cueva (€€)
Cave-like ambience in this unique Carmona restaurant. Excellent Andalucían cuisine. Try *albornla*, a mix of fried vegetables, or *aliños*, a crispy fresh salad. Desserts include boiled chestnuts with cinnamon.

- ✉ Barbacana Baja 2 ☎ 954 19 18 11 🕐 Lunch and dinner

Ecija
Bodegon del Gallego (€€)
Located just round the corner from the Palacio de Peñaflor, this popular and well-run restaurant offers good fish dishes. Pick your own lobster, if you can bear to, from a display tank. Reservations advised.

- ✉ c/ Arcipreste Aparicio 3
- ☎ 954 83 26 18
- 🕐 Lunch and dinner

Huelva
Taberna El Condado (€)
Lively tapas bar in the old part of town. Rustic flavour. Popular with locals.

- ✉ Calle Sor Ángela de la Cruz 3 ☎ 959 26 11 23 🕐 Lunch and dinner. Closed Sun

Moguer
Meson el Lobito (€)
One of the most fascinating eating places in Andalucía, El Lobito is housed in a cavernous building, the walls of which are dense with the graffiti of patrons' names and initials. Cobwebbed and soot-encased oddments hang from the rafters. Alongside the bar is a huge open fire, on which food is expertly grilled.

- ✉ c/ Rábida 31 ☎ 959 37 06 60 🕐 Lunch and dinner

Osuna

Casa Curro (€)

Excellent *tapas* bar and a good standard menu in this pleasant bar-restaurant in a small attractive square. A local favourite.

Plaza Salitre 5–9 955 82 07 58 Breakfast, lunch, dinner. Closed Mon

Doña Guadalupe (€)

Popular restaurant situated on a small square. It has a good reputation for its cuisine and a pleasant patio for outdoor eating.

Plaza Guadalupe 6 954 81 05 58 Lunch and dinner. Closed Tue

Seville

Casa Robles (€€)

Family-run restaurant dating from the early fifties, a short walk from the cathedral,The *azulejo*-clad walls are typically Andaluz – as is the cuisine, including fish soup, hake and Serrano ham, plus tempting desserts.

Calle Álvarez Quintero 58 954 21 31 50 Lunch and dinner

Corral del Agua (€ €€)

Housed in a former 18th-century mansion in the Santa Cruz district this restaurant features a delightful plant-filled courtyard for dining out in the summer. Andalucían-style dishes.

Callejón del Agua 6 954 22 48 41 Lunch and dinner. Closed Sun, Jan and Feb

La Cueva (€€)

Patio restaurant at the heart of the Santa Cruz area. Excellent fish dishes, *paella* and lamb specialities.

c/ Rodrigo Caro 18 954 21 31 43 Lunch and dinner

Enrique Becerra (€€)

Attractive eatery with an international reputation, between Plaza Nueva and the bullring. Try the *salad de pàte et crabe* (pasta and spider crab salad), or roasted lamb with honey and spinach and pine seed stuffing.

c/ Gamazo 2 954 21 30 49 Lunch and dinner. Closed Sun

El Giraldillo (€€)

Great *tapas* selection in this popular restaurant in sight of Seville's cathedral. Try the eggs 'flamenco style', a subtle mix of eggs, tomatoes, garlic onions and salami. Excellent *gazpacho*.

Plaza Virgen de los Reyes 2 954 21 45 25 Lunch and dinner

Hotel Alfonso XIII (€€€)

Dining here demands serious money, but the surroundings might just make you feel like a millionaire. Lunch is less of a drain on resources and offers an excellent choice.

c/ San Fernando 2 954 91 70 00 Lunch and dinner

Modesto (€)

Great fish and seafood restaurant in the southeast of Santa Cruz. Outside terrace where you can enjoy a good selection of *tapas* and *raciónes* from the menu.

c/ Cano y Cueto 5 954 41 68 11 Lunch and dinner

El Rincón de Pepe (€€)

Located in a handsome 19th-century house at the heart of Santa Cruz. Fine *azulejos* tiling in dining room and there is a patio. Noted for *paella* and fried fish dishes.

c/Gloria 6 954 56 29 75 Lunch and dinner

Choosing What To Eat

Restaurants usually offer a fixed-price menu of the day, called *menú del día* or *menú de la casa*. This will usually be a two- or three-course meal with bread and wine and will cost from €10 to €19. Confusingly for North Europeans, a list showing a selection of dishes at a restaurant is called *la carta*, not a *menú*. Ask for *la carta* if you want to make your own selection. A meal from *la carta* costs more than the *menú del día*.

Tapas Tip

Tapas for vegetarians to look out for include *aceitunas* (olives), *habas* (broad beans) *ensaladilla* (salad, often with dressing), *berenjenas con miel* (fried slices of aubergine with honey), *pisto* (vegetable stew), *patatas ali-oli* (fried potatoes in garlic mayonnaise), *huevos revueltos* (scrambled egg), and *queso* (cheese).

Córdoba & Jaén

Prices

Prices are for a double room, excluding breakfast and VAT:
€ = under €60
€€ = €60–€150
€€€ = over €150

Choice of Stay

The main distinctions between accommodation options in Andalucía are between *fondas*, *pensiones* (pensions), *hostales* (hostels) and *hoteles* (hotels). *Fondas*, with an 'F' sign, and *pensiones*, with a 'P' sign, are inexpensive and can be quite basic, but are often more than adequate and can sometimes supply meals. Hostels, marked with an 'H' sign, are often quite numerous in larger towns and cities. They can also be inexpensive and usually have a mix of en suite rooms and rooms with a shared bathroom. Standards vary, but some hostals can be excellent value and full of character. The better ones may have air conditioning. Hotels are graded from one to five stars. Below three stars, there is often little distinction between hotels and *hostals*. Above three stars, hotels become significantly more expensive and you will find the same facilities and service that you would expect to find in similarly starred hotels throughout Europe.

Baeza

Hospedería Fuentenueva (€€)

Charming 12-bedroom hotel, once a prison – now transformed by sophisticated décor and furnishings. Regular art exhibitions. Excellent restaurant.

📧 **Avenida Puche Pardo s/n**
☎ **953 74 31 00;**
www.fuentenueva.com

Cazorla

Hotel Guadalquivir (€€)

A pleasant hotel located at the heart of the town between Plaza Corredera and Plaza Santa Maria.

📧 **c/ Nueva 6** ☎ **953 72 02 68; fax 953 72 02 68**

Córdoba

Hotel Maestre (€)

Smart, modern hotel with bright and airy patios. Adjoinining is the slightly cheaper Hostal Maestre, under the same management. The company also has apartments to let.

📧 **c/ Romero Barros 4–6** ☎ **957 47 24 10; fax 957 47 53 95**

Hotel Mezquita (€€)

Conveniently opposite the Mosque. Former 16th-century mansion, restored in typical Spanish style, with a charming courtyard.

📧 **Plaza Catalina** ☎ **957 47 55 85**

Hotel Los Omeyas (€€)

Located in the heart of the 'Judería', the old quarter of the city, only a few steps from the Mezquita and other attractions. Arab motifs throughout, including a traditional courtyard patio.

📧 **c/ Encarnacion 17**
☎ **957 49 22 67/21 27;**
fax 957 49 16 59

Jaen

Hotel Xauen (€€)

Just off the Plaza de la Constitución. Rooms have air-conditioning. Self-service coffee shop. Parking.

📧 **Plaza de Deán Mazas 3**
☎ **953 24 07 89;**
www.hotelxauenjan.com

Priego de Córdoba

Hostal Rafi (€)

At the bottom end of the price range, this delightful hostal lies in a narrow street near the Plaza de la Constitución.

📧 **Isabel la Católica 4** ☎ **957 54 07 49; fax 957 54 70 27**

Segura de la Sierra

Los Huertos de Segura (€€)

At the village's highest point with apartments for 2 to 4 people, with bathroom, kitchenette, open fireplace and magnificent views. Welcoming atmosphere. Restaurant close by.

📧 **Calle Castillo 11**
☎ **953 48 04 02; www.rurtal.com-loshuertodesegura**

Úbeda

Parador de Úbeda (€€)

Charming location in the handsome Plaza de Vázquez de Molina. Originally a 16th-century palace, the *parador* retains many period features, including inner courtyard with galleries and rooms with high ceilings.

📧 **Plaza de Vázquez Molina s/n** ☎ **953 75 03 45;**
www.parador.es

Zuheros

Hotel Zuhayra (€€)

Delightful little hotel with its own pool and patio. Tasty local dishes in the restaurant.

📧 **c/ Mirador 10**
☎ **957 69 46 93**

Granada & Almería

Alhama de la Granada

Balneario de Alhama de Granada (€€)

Long-established spa hotel built over preserved Moorish baths. The hotel has a rather plain appearance, which is compensated by its attractive, riverside location among trees. Thermal baths and other health treatments are available.

✉ Ctra del Balneario s/n
☎ 958 35 00 11/03 66;
fax 958 35 02 97

Almería

Gran Hotel Almería (€€€)

Luxury hotel located at the seaward end of the Rambla de Belén. Close to the old town but out of Puerta de Purchena focus, although it makes up for it with its own disco and swimming pool.

✉ Avda Reina Regente 8
☎ 950 23 80 11;
www.granhotelalmeria.com

Hotel la Perla (€€)

Said to be the oldest hotel in Almería; family-run. Located just off the Puerta Purchena's busy square, the liveliest part of town, but detached enough from too much street noise.

✉ Plaza del Carmen 7
☎ 950 23 88 77; fax 950 27 58 16

Hotel Torreluz III/Hotel Torreluz II (€€–€€€)

Two hotels in attractive square, and under same management. Hotel Torreluz II is the more expensive and stylish. Hotel Torreluz is of the same basic standard but is in a more anonymous building. Both are associated with excellent restaurants. (There is a third Torreluz

hotel in the square. This is AM Torreluz; independent of and more expensive than its namesakes.

✉ Plaza Flores 3 (Torreluz III);
Plaza Flores 6 (Torreluz II)
☎ 950 23 43 99;
www.torreluz.com (both hotels)

Bérchules

La Posada (€)

Excellent base for exploring Las Alpujarras. Authentic Alpujarras-style house, hundreds of years old, at the heart of Berchules. Evening meal and breakfast. Local 'house' wine recommended. English spoken by friendly proprietors.

✉ Plaza del Ayuntamiento s/n
☎ 958 85 25 41

Bubión

Villa Turística del Poqueira (€€)

Purpose-built hotel of 43 houses built as replicas of traditional Alpujarran dwellings, all with terrace or private garden.

✉ Barrio Alto s/n
☎ 958 76 39 09

Granada

Hotel Carmen (€€€)

Luxurious hotel in the centre of Granada, with all facilities. Special suites, including nuptial suite. Pool terrace with great views. Jewellery and fashion shops for those with the money to spare.

✉ Acera del Darro 62 ☎ 958 25 83 00; www.hotelcarmen.com

Hotel Macía Plaza (€€)

On Plaza Nueva. Excellent location for visiting Granada's major attractions. Some rooms have a good view over this lively square.

✉ Plaza Nueva
☎ 958 22 75 36

Safety and Security

Most types of accommodation in Andalucía have a watchful eye looking over them – if not the proprietor's, then a member of staff's. However, you should either take valuable items with you when going out, or make use of the establishment's safe, if it has one. If you have hired a car it is much more likely to be a target for theft. If you leave the car parked, ensure there is nothing visble on the back seat.

Many *hostals* and hotels may have lifts without a closing cabin door, and the wall of the lift well is therefore unguarded as it travels up or down. Great care should be taken of young children in such lifts. If you have any legitimate complaint about your accommodation, ask for the *libro de reclamaciones* (official complaints book). This must be kept by law and should be inspected regularly by the police.

Granada & Almería

The Old, the New, and the Luxurious

In cities there is a mix of old-fashioned and modern hotels. Hotels on the coast tend to be high-rise and modern. Top of the tree are *paradores*. These are state-run hotels often located in magnificent buildings such as Moorish castles or palaces which have been luxuriously converted. Others are custom-built. All offer the highest standards and luxury, but have prices to match. If you want more remote accommodation with character, try the central booking service for cottages, farmhouses, refuges and other rural dwellings, the Red Andaluza de Alojamiento Rural, ☎ 902 44 22 23; www.raar.es. As well as *paradores* there are state-run Villas Turísticas, complexes of luxury self-catering apartments or cottages that have all the central facilities of top hotels. For information contact Turismo Andaluz ☎ 952 12 93 00; fax 952 12 93 15; www.andalucia.org

Hotel Los Tilos (€€)
A traditional no-frills hotel overlooking a bustling plaza with a daily flower market and plenty of café choice.
✉ **Plaza Bib-Rambla 4**
☎ **958 26 67 12**

Parador de Granada (€€€)
Very expensive, top-of-the-range hotel – also top-of-the-hill, with its outstanding location at the heart of the Alhambra. Beautiful surroundings incorporate Moorish features. Reservations are strongly advised.
✉ **Real de la Alhambra s/n**
☎ **958 22 14 40;**
www.parador.es

Guadix
Hotel Comercio (€€)
Prize-winning hotel dating from 1901, beautifully refurbished. Comfortable rooms, lounges and restaurants serving top local and international cuisine.
✉ **c/ Mira de Amezcua, 3**
☎ **958 66 05 00;**
fax 958 66 50 72

Laujar De Andarax
Villa Turística de Laujar (€€€)
Luxurious and expensive modern hotel set in its own large grounds and with every facility. A good base for exploring the eastern section of Las Alpujarras. Own restaurant with Andalucían and local specialities.
✉ **Cortijo de la Villa** ☎ **950 51 30 27; www.naturahotels.com**

Mojácar
Parador de Mojácar (€€€)
Very luxurious hotel complex on Mojácar's sea front. The busy main road passes the gates and you have to cross this road to reach the far-from-exclusive beach. However, the hotel has real exclusivity and luxurious facilities, including a swimming pool that you need never leave.
✉ **Playa de Mojácar** ☎ **950 47 82 50; www.parador.es**

Montefrío
Hotel La Enrea (€€)
A very pleasant new hotel with modern facilities and excellent service.
✉ **Paraje la Enrea s/n** ☎ **958 33 66 62; fax 958 33 67 96**

Solynieve (Sierra Nevada)
Meliá Sierra Nevada (€€€)
Most of Solynieve's hotels and hostals close during the summer and autumn, skiing being their main source of custom.
✉ **Pradallano s/n** ☎ **958 48 04 00; fax 958 48 04 58**

Trevélez
Hotel la Fragua
Well-placed hotel giving good views of surrounding slopes and with pleasant, well-appointed rooms. A bonus is the hotel's own restaurant nearby, the Méson la Fragua.
✉ **c/ San Antoni 4** ☎ **958 85 86 26; fax 958 85 86 14**

Vélez Blanco
Hostal la Sociedad (€)
Excellent value at this modern, well-appointed *hostal*. Enquire at the emphatically 'local' Bar Sociedad, in the main square, a few metres along the main road.
✉ **c/ Corredera 7**
☎ **950 41 50 27**

Málaga & Cádiz

Antequera

Parador de Antequera (€€)

Modern *parador* with all the luxury and good service associated with *paradors*. Surrounded by attractive gardens. Excellent restaurant and various activities and excursions organised.

✉ **Paseo García del Olmo s/n**
☎ **952 84 02 61;**
fax 952 84 13 12

Arcos de la Frontera

Hotel La Fonda (€)

A delightful hotel in the busy lower town, but within easy reach of the old centre. La Fonda was originally a coaching inn, dating from the mid-19th century. Its restaurant is in the converted stables. High ceilings, wooden galleries and hand-made tiling all add to the atmosphere.

✉ **c/ Corredera 83** ☎ **956 70 00 57; www.cogh.com/lafonda**

Los Olivos (€€)

Delightful, small hotel right in the heart of the old town. All modern facilities, yet with traditional style reflected in its beautiful patio. Hotel restaurant is recommended for excellent local cuisine.

✉ **San Miguel 2, Boliches**
☎ **956 70 08 11**

Parador de Arcos de la Frontera (€€€)

A prime location on the Plaza del Cabildo adds to the cachet of this luxury *parador*. Moorish and Mudéjar décor and furnishings throughout, and fine views from many of the balconied rooms. The restaurant serves traditional local cuisine.

✉ **Plaza del Cabildo s/n**
☎ **956 70 05 00;**
fax 956 70 11 16

Cadíz

Hostal Fantoni (€)

This delightful small *hostal* is tucked away in an otherwise dull side street off Plaza Juan de Dios. Marble staircases and *azulejos* tiles every-where. Small but spotless rooms. Hugely popular, so reservations advised.

✉ **Flamenco 5**
☎ **956 28 27 04**

Hostal Bahia (€)

Excellent-value small pension near the central Plaza de San Juan de Dios. Most rooms have balconies and all are attractively furnished with modern bathrooms. Recommended restaurant, Mesón La Nueva Marina, right next door.

✉ **Calle Plocia 5** ☎ **956 25 90 61; fax 956 25 42 08**

Parador Hotel Atlántico (€€€)

Overlooking the sea and with direct access to the beach, this classic *parador* has all the luxurious facilities of its kind. Good restaurant offering traditional and international cuisine.

✉ **Avda Duque de Nájera 9**
☎ **956 22 69 05;**
fax 956 21 45 82

Gibraltar

Bristol (€€)

A smart, mid-price hotel, but still near the top end of the range, quality-wise – like most things in Gibraltar. Good location, near the cathedral, and with its own garden and pool.

✉ **10 Cathedral Square**
☎ **350 76800; fax 350 77613**

Travellers with Disabilities

There are few facilities for travellers with disabilities in Andalucía, but the situation may well improve as the authorities and the tourism business grow more aware of the need for them. It is already noticeable that more hotels are installing ramps, special lifts and other facilities for travellers with disabilities. For further information contact Las Gerencias Provinciales del Instituto Andaluz de Servicios Sociales (The Provincial Management of the Andalucían Institute of Social Services), Avenida Manuel Augustín 26, Málaga ☎ 952 12 96 00

Driving Maze

When looking for somewhere to stay in villages and small towns, resist the temptation to drive along ever-narrowing streets. If you are not sure where they are leading, you may end up like a cork in a bottle. If reversing round tight corners of narrow streets, check that the kerb is not as high as a small wall; otherwise the first you will know of it is a loud grinding noise. Except during *siesta*, If you do get stuck across a narrow junction of village streets and no one is around, brace yourself. From all directions, a blaring cacophony of cars, vans, lorries, motorbikes, scooters, the occasional donkey plus amused pedestrians offering advice in quick-fire Spanish, is guaranteed to materialise within seconds.

Grazalema
Villa Turística de Grazalema (€€€)
Near the village of Grazalema in fine surroundings, this luxury hotel has good facilities enhanced by its own gardens, pool and restaurant.
✉ **Ctra. Comercal 344** ☎ **956 13 21 36; fax 956 13 22 13**

Jerez de la Frontera
El Ancla Hotel (€)
Delightful small hotel in typical Andalucían building with wrought-iron balconies and yellow paintwork.Rooms are plainly furnished but clean and comfortable; underground parking near by.
✉ **Plaza del Mamelón** ☎ **956 32 12 97; fax 956 32 50 05**

Málaga
Hotel Venecia (€)
Central location on Málaga's main avenue, down by the Plaza de la Marina. Basic facilities, spacious rooms. Good value.
✉ **Alameda Principal 9** ☎ **952 21 36 36**

Larios (€€€)
Smart hotel in the city centre's most fashionable shopping street, near the cathedral. Black-and-white tiles, cool beige furnishings and pine make for a modern, upbeat look. Some of the rooms overlook the lovely Plaza de la Constitución.
✉ **Marqués de Larios 2** ☎ **952 22 22 00; fax 952 22 24 07**

Málaga-Gibralfaro (€€€)
Splendid *parador* located high above the town on the Gibralfaro hill, with glorious views across the bay.
✉ **Castillo de Gibralfaro s/n** ☎ **952 22 19 02; fax 952 22 19 04; www.parador.es**

Nerja
Hotel Balcón de Europa (€€)
Located at the heart of Nerja, adjoining the 'Balcón de Europa' and with access to Caletilla Beach.
✉ **Paseo Balcón de Europa 1** ☎ **952 52 08 00; fax 952 52 44 90**

Ronda
Hotel Don Miguel (€€)
A comfortable small hotel with pleasant rooms and some spectacular views of Ronda's famous gorge.
✉ **Plaza Espanna 4** ☎ **952 87 77 22; fax 952 87 83 77**

Parador de Ronda (€€€)
Ronda's 18th-century town hall now functions as a lavishly restored and delightful *parador* with many of its rooms overlooking the Tajo, the deep gorge that has made Ronda famous.
✉ **Plaza de España s/n** ☎ **952 87 75 00; fax 952 87 81 88**

Sanlúcar de Barrameda
Los Helechos (€€)
Mid-size hotel in converted *bodega* near bus station and centre of town. Well-maintained and comfortable rooms arranged round two patios.
✉ **Plaza Madres de Dios 9** ☎ **956 36 76 55; fax 956 36 96 50**

Tarifa
Hurricane Hotel (€€)
Wonderful, if wind-swept hotel on the beach; a favourite among windsurfers.
✉ **Carretera Cádiz-Málaga km 77** ☎ **956 68 49 19; fax 956 68 43 29**

Zahara de la Sierra
Arco de la Villa (€€)
Small, modern hotel in an enviable position on Zahara's rocky outcrop.To reach it, go all the way through the village and then continue uphill towards the castle.
✉ **Camino Nazari s/n** ☎ **956 12 32 30; fax 956 12 32 44**

Seville & Huelva

Aracena
Finca Valbono (€€)
Situated in pleasant surroundings just outside Aracena, this old farmhouse has been tastefully converted into a small hotel with a restaurant, pool and riding stables.

 Carretera de Carboneras, Km 1 ☎ 959 12 77 11

Aroche
Hostal Picos de Aroche (€)
It's worth the trip to Aroche for a stay in this friendly and immaculate establishment.

✉ **Ctra Aracena 12**
☎ 959 14 04 75/18

Carmona
Pensión El Comercio (€)
Attractive, small *pension* built into the walls of the Puerta de Sevilla, the magnificent western gateway to the town.

✉ **c/ Torre del Oro 56**
☎ 954 14 00 18

Huelva
Luz Huelva (€€€)
Top end of the price scale at this large, luxurious hotel near the museum and railway station.

✉ **Alameda Sundheim 26**
☎ 959 25 00 11; fax 959 25 81 10

Moguer
Hostal Pedro Alonso Niño (€)
Outstanding value at this delightful little *hostal* with its immaculate tiled patio and comfortable ensuite rooms with TV. Friendly owners.

✉ **c/ Pedro Alonso Niño 13**
☎ 959 37 23 92

Hostal Platero (€)
Pleasant *hostal* named after the hero of Juan Ramón Jimenez's famous book

(► 14) and close to the centre of the town.

✉ **c/ Aceña 4** ☎ 959 37 21 59

Osuna
El Caballo Blanco (€€)
This old coaching inn, a fascinating building, retains its arched entranceway and stableyard, where guests park their cars – a great advantage here. Pleasant rooms and good restaurant.

✉ **c/ Granada 1**
☎ 954 81 01 84

Seville
Hotel Alfonso XIII (€€€€)
Very expensive, luxurious world-class hotel, custom-built in 1928 and still a focus of rich living. The stylised Moorish interiors are the last word in elegance and lavishness and there is an excellent restaurant open to non-residents.

✉ **San Fernando 2** ☎ 954 91 70 00; fax 954 91 70 99

Hotel Amadeus (€€)
Former 18th-century mansion, beautifully restored and decorated. With pianos in several soundproof rooms and concerts sometimes held in the foyer, this small hotel draws in musicians and music lovers. Terrace offers good views

✉ **Calle Farnesio**
☎ 954 50 14 43

Hotel Simón (€€)
A well-placed city-centre hotel, just off the Avenue de la Constitución and near the cathedral. Once a private mansion, the hotel retains its period style, with handsome patio and staircases.

✉ **c/ García de Vinuesa 19**
☎ 954 22 66 60;
fax 954 56 22 41

Parking
Many hotels and some *hostals* have their own parking, but finding a place to park in Andalucían towns and villages can sometimes be a nightmare. Car parks are either non-existent or obscure in most places and central parking, especially in the mornings and late afternoons, is at a premium, amid quite hectic traffic. It is often best to find stress-free, street-side parking at the first convenient opportunity as you enter a town or village, depending on its size. This may entail a bit of a walk to the centre, but you can then assess more central parking and drive to it later.

Arts, Crafts, Gifts and Antiques

Souvenirs

Big cities and major attractions in Andalucía are well served by souvenir shops. Andalucía has a great tradition of craftwork, and in many quieter corners of cities, and certainly in provincial towns and villages, you will find shops, workshops and studios selling marvellous artefacts. For pottery and tiles, try Úbeda, Níjar and Sorbas. In Córdoba, look for Andalucían jewellery, the finest leather goods, guitars and embroidery. Jaén province is noted for wicker and woven crafts using esparto and other grasses; Úbeda also has several outlets, as does Guadix, in Granada province, and Almería city. Granada has numerous outlets for tapestry work and is also a noted centre of marquetry, a craft dating from Moorish times. Seville has many goldsmiths, silversmiths and potteries. You will find blankets and ponchos and other textile craft at Grazalema and Níjar.

Gifts and Antiques

Almería

La Tienda de los Milagros
This is one of the best places to go if you want to take home some of the distinctive local pottery produced by local workshops in the Barrio Alfarero (Potter's Quarter).
✉ **Calle Lavadero 2 (Nijar)**
☎ **950 36 03 59**

Granada

Casa Ferrer
Possibly the best-known music store in the province, dating from 1875; their stock includes an elegant assortment of hand-crafted guitars.
✉ **Cuesta de Gomérez 20**
☎ **956 22 18 32**

Gonzálo Reyes Muñoz
A fascinating antiques shop with a strong Spanish element, which should intrigue collectors and casual buyers alike. You'll find enough fine smaller pieces to choose from if you don't have room in your case for some hefty furniture.
✉ **c/ Mesones (Placeta de Cauchiles 1)** ☎ **958 52 32 74**

Mima
A very traditional shop selling *mantones* (gowns), *mantillas* (veils), *abanicos* (fans) and *tejido* (fabric). Courteous and friendly service. English and French is spoken.
✉ **Reyes Catolicos 18**
☎ **958 22 40 74**

Ruiz Linares
This is the place to come for a great mix of antiques and *objéts d'art* including paintings, sculptures, toys, and jewellery.
✉ **Zacatín 21** ☎ **958 22 23 47**

Sombrero Trecabado
The ultimate place to make for if you forget your sun hat, or if you fancy another one. All types of hats, caps and Andalucían sombreros are on sale in this fine, old-fashioned shop. Unusually, they are not on the telephone.
✉ **Zacatín 24**

Jerez de la Frontera

Calle del Flamenco
Everything connected with *flamenco* in this fascinating shop in the Barrio de Santiago district. There are flamenco rehearsal rooms here, too.
✉ **c/ Francos 49**
☎ **956 34 01 39**

Art and Crafts

Alhama de Granada

Artesanía los Tajos
A fine little gallery-shop selling arts and craft work from the local area. Located in a delightful position, close to the Iglesia del Carmen.
✉ **c/ Peña 34** ☎ **958 36 01 64**

Aracena

Artesanía Pascual
A wonderful craft shop with a fascinating range of artefacts and potential gifts, and a friendly owner. You'll find it just behind the car park.
✉ **Plaza de San Pedro 47**
☎ **959 12 80 07**

Arcos de la Frontera

Galería de Arte, Arx-Arcis
Attractive gallery at the heart of the old town with a good selection of paintings, ceramics, *esparto* work, rugs and other traditional artefacts.
✉ **c/ Marqués de Torresoto 11**
☎ **956 70 39 51**

Córdoba

Artesanía Cordobesa

A celebrated shop for leather goods and other artefacts, including an excellent selection of hand-made ceramics, including ornaments, kitchenware and tiles.

✉ Calle Romero 10
☎ 957 29 03 84

El Zoco

A fascinating jewellery market in the heart of the Jewish quarter, with several shops, most of which specialise in the distinctive filigree silverware.

✉ Avenida de Gran Capitán
☎ No telephone

Montefrio

Pedro Romero Ruiz

This is one of those Andalucían village shops selling virtually everything. The place to get your genuine sombrero, as worn by local farmers.

✉ General Franco 2

Osuna

Ferretería Arte

An astonishing collection of rural and domestic ironmongery that is worth a browse even if you don't need anything.

✉ Carrera 17–19
☎ 954 81 09 07

Seville

Arteanía Textil

Fascinating shop selling an intriguing selection of gift items, such as wall hangings, hand-embroidered tablecloths and place mats.

✉ Calle Sierpes 70
☎ 954 56 28 40

Modas Muñoz

The place for Sevillian dress, if you fancy *mantoncillos*, flamenco scarves and veils, shawls and shoes to get your heels tapping.

✉ Cerrajería 5
☎ 954 22 85 96

Ceramics

Carmona

Cerámica San Blas

Fine, working pottery tucked away down a quiet side street, complete with modern pottery oven that radiates even more heat just inside the entrance door.

✉ c/ Dominguez de la Haza 18
☎ 954 14 40 49;
fax 954 14 40 49

Granada

González Ramos, Taller de Taracea

One of the best of several workshop-galleries producing marquetry (*taracea*).

✉ Cuesta de Gomerez 16
☎ 958 22 20 70

Níjar

La Tienda de los Milagros

Outstanding ceramics with bright, colourful designs and glazes. Skilfully blending traditional craft with modern ideas.

✉ c/ Lavadero 2
☎ 950 36 03 59 (shop);
950 52 57 51 (workshop)

Sorbas

Alfarería Juan Simon

Family-run workshop and shop in the lower town, at the heart of the pottery-making district.

✉ c/ Alfarerías 25
☎ 950 36 40 83

Seville

Azulejos Santa Isabel

Superb ceramics shop in the Triana district of Seville, south of the river.

✉ Alfarería 12
☎ 954 34 46 08

Úbeda

Alfarería Gongora

This well-known potter has his shop in the 'street of potters' in Úbeda – a town famous for its attractive dark green pottery.

✉ c/ Cuesta de la Merced 32
☎ 953 75 46 05

Begging

You will need to get used to being approached in Andalucían cities by all types of people asking for money or cigarettes. Many beggars are businesslike, rattling through a crowded café terrace at a great pace, in order to avoid being seen off by quick-footed waiters, but also to cover as many people as possible. Outside major sights you may be approached by gypsies offering sprigs of rosemary. If you do not wish to buy, do not engage in conversation or make eye contact; move on with purpose. As always, in crowded places, guard your pockets and bags.

Children's, Fashion and Books

Local Information

Andalucía is becoming increasingly sophisticated in terms of tourism promotion, but there are sometimes huge variations in the kind of information available locally. Quite rightly, many areas of Andalucía cater for Spanish tourists first, and you may find that in some provincial towns and villages most, if not all, leaflets, brochures, local guidebooks and town and village maps are in Spanish, and that staff speak only Spanish. Many staff, however, do speak at least a little English.

Children's Shops

Almería
Carrusel
Shoes of all shades and styles for children are on offer in this bright, colourful and friendly little shop.
✉ **Tenor Iribarne 11**

Cádiz
Quentum
Great selection of colourful and diverting children's toys, books and other goods.
✉ **Plaza de Mina 13** ☎ **956 22 50 11; fax 956 22 76 07**

Fashion

Cádiz
Tosso
Stylish bags, fans, hats and every other decorative accessory you can think of, all in quality materials.
✉ **Palillero 4** ☎ **956 21 14 98**

Córdoba
Modas Pilar Morales
A rather chic dress shop between Plaza de las Tendillas and the Avenida del Gran Capitán. Assistants have just the right touch of Córdoban hauteur.
✉ **Conde de Gondomar 2** ☎ **957 47 12 54**

Granada
Roberto Verino
Very stylish, very cool fashion salon for both men's and women's wear.
✉ **Reyes Catolicos 23** ☎ **958 21 50 43**

Malaga
Mango
Good-sized branch of this hugely successful national (and international) chain. Clothes are well-made and smart, ranging from snazzy suits to summer dresses
✉ **Larios 1** ☎ **952 22 31 02**

Puerto Banús
Donna Piu
Exciting fashions from Italian designer collections, to go with the general high fashion look in this trendy resort.
✉ **Benabola** ☎ **952 81 49 90**

Seville
Agua de Sevilla
Very stylish perfumery and accessories shop tucked away in Santa Cruz and near the Alcázar.
✉ **Rodrigo Caro 16** ☎ **954 21 06 54**

Swear
Footwear, streetwear, and the latest in fashion trends for teens and their parents.
✉ **Reyes Católicos** ☎ **954 56 39 25**

Book Shops

Granada
Librería Dauro
A good little book shop with all types of books.
✉ **Zacatin 3** ☎ **958 22 45 21; fax 958 22 91 46**

Nerja
Nerja Book and Video Centre
A big selection of second-hand books in various languages; videos for rent.
✉ **c/Granada 30** ☎ **952 52 09 08**

Seville
Vértice
International book shop in the university area of Seville. Maps, guides and general books in many languages.
✉ **c/ San Fernando 33** ☎ **954 21 16 54**

Jewellery, Food & Drink

Jewellery

Cádiz
Arco
This is one of those tucked-away shops with some appealing jewellery and accessories. It also does a charming line in mobile phones.
✉ c/ San José 23
☎ 956 22 30 71

Fuengirola
Nicholson
Fashionable jewellery products and accessories, including earrings and bracelets.
✉ c/ Marbella s/n
☎ 952 47 58 82

Granada
Luis Berkem
A small, stylish jewellery shop with some subtle pieces. Tucked away in an alleyway near Reyes Catolicos.
✉ c/ Monterería 11
☎ 958 25 01 31

Jerez
Joyería Monaco
A wide selection of jewellery, gold and silver work, as well as porcelain and crystalware.
✉ Larga 17 ☎ 956 33 18 37

Seville
Casa Ruiz
High-quality jewellery and silverware in two shops.
✉ O'Donnell 14 ☎ 954 22 21 37/21 25 96; fax 954 21 12 16
✉ Sierpes 68 ☎ 954 22 77 80

Food And Drink

Aracena
Jamones y Embeutidos Ibéricos, La Trastiendsa
The real *jamón negra* or *pata negra* of the Sierra Morena is on sale here, as well as a range of other speciality Spanish meat products including *morcilla* (blood sausage), *chorizo* (spicy sausage) and *salchichon* (a salami variety of sausage).
✉ Plaza San Pedro 2
☎ 959 12 71 58/87 96

Granada
Lopez-Mezquita
Mouth-watering and eye-catching displays in this *cafetería-pastelería* offering a huge array of sweet delicacies to tempt even the most jaded.
✉ Reyes Catolicos 39–41
☎ 958 22 12 05

Malaga
La Mallorquina
One of the city's many wonderful delicatessens with a mouth-watering window display of great wheels of *Manchego* cheese, cold cuts, nuts, dried fruits and locally produced *turrón* (nougat) and marzipan.
This is also the place to pick up your Málaga wine made from sweet muscatel grapes.
✉ Plaza de Félix Sáenz
☎ No telephone

Trevélez
Jamones y Embutidos Chorrillo
If you want to find the best in Alpujarran *jamón*, said to be perfected in the clean air of the mountains, then this Sierra Nevada company has a quarter of a century of experience.
✉ Guadalupe Exposito. Haza de la Iglesia s/n
☎ 958 85 86 85

Spanish Fashion
In the streets of Andalucía's main cities, and especially in stylish Seville, you will find fashion shops selling all the top brand names of Europe and America, as well as such increasingly-known chains as Mango and Zara. For something essentially Andalucían, however, flamenco fashion is the ultimate. Though the flounced dresses in bright polka dot and floral patterns were once considered vulgar by Andalucían established society, today such costume is proudly worn by countless Andalucíans during the great festivals and at numerous other events. The flamenco style is also replicated in contemporary fashion. You can buy items of flamenco costume in a number of shops, especially in Seville, Granada and Córdoba. But remember, it takes a certain panache to wear it well.

1

Children's Activities

Fun and Games

The Costa del Sol is for fun and games. There are a number of water parks to complement the Costa's numerous beaches and here adults can relax as much as youngsters do. The sheer pace of life on the Costa del Sol, its shops, cafés and restaurants, the crowds and the numerous attractions are all diverting for youngsters, but inland Andalucía has other attractions. Horse riding is an excellent activity for all the family. Above all, you should find out if there is a festival near you. Spanish children play a major part in such events and children on holiday will be fascinated by it all.

Almería
Mini Hollywood

Near Tabernas on the A370, this is the desert hills location for Sergio Leone's famous 'Spaghetti Western' *A Fistful of Dollars*, and for subsequent, similar films. Now a full-blooded Western theme park, with the old sets convincingly realistic, until you peep behind the façades. Tombstone Gulch saloon is substantially real – there are staged gunfights at High Noon, and a second shift at 5PM from mid-June to mid-September. Great fun all round. There is also a safari wild animal park, the Reserva Zoologica near by.

✉ **Ctra Nacional 340-km**
☎ **950 36 52 36 (Mini Hollywood); 950 36 29 31 (Reserva Zoologica)**

Granada
Parque de las Ciencias (Science Park)

Great fun as well as being informative, the Science Park has numerous hands-on features and ingenious interactive experiences. There is an observatory and planetarium to add to the interest.

✉ **Avenida del Mediterráneo s/n** ☎ **958 13 19 00**
🕐 **Tue–Sat 10–7, Sun 10–3**
🚌 **5** 🦽 **Good**
🖥 **Moderate**

Jerez
Parque Zoologico (Botanical Gardens and Zoo)

A pleasant facility with a good record of environmentalism and preservation. Various wild animals, many of which are cared for after being injured. The gardens are delightful.

✉ **c/ Taxdirt s/n**
☎ **956 18 23 97/42 07; fax 956 31 15 86** 🕐 **Tue–Sun 10–6**
🚌 **9** 🦽 **Fair** 🖥 **Moderate**

Yeguada de la Cartuja Hierra del Bocado Stud

Paradise for horse-mad youngsters – and for everyone, in fact. State-owned stud where thoroughbred horses are carefully bred and raised. Open days enable visitors to see the horses in action, drawing carriages and going through training. Reservations are advised and can be made by phone or through hotels.

✉ **Finca Fuente El Suero, Ctra Medina-El Portal 6.5 km**
☎ **956 16 28 09;**
fax 956 16 28 22 🕐 **Sat only, 11AM** 🖥 **Expensive**

Tarifa
Whales and Dolphins and Whale Watch

Go pilot whale and dolphin-spotting from fast boats in the Strait of Gibraltar. It's an exciting day out even though a glimpse of these fine creatures is not guaranteed. Companies running these include:

FIRMM
✉ **Calle Pedro Cortés 4**
☎ **956 70 08**

Whale Watch
✉ **Café Continental, Paseo de la Alameda**
☎ **956 68 22 47** 🖥 **Expensive**

Costa del Sol

Benalmádena
Tivoli World

The ultimate Costa del Sol amusement park. Funfair rides galore, water flume,

Wild West town, open-air theatre, mock Spanish 'plaza', live entertainment. Over a dozen cafés and restaurants cater for all tastes. Very popular during the summer season and busy at weekends, especially.

✉ **Avenida del Tivoli, Arroyo de la Miel** ☎ **952 57 70 16** 🕐 **Apr, May, 15–30 Sep, Oct 4PM–1AM; Jun, 1–14 Sep 5PM–2AM; Jul, Aug 6PM–3AM; Nov–Mar 11AM–9PM** 🍴 **Numerous cafés and restaurants (€–€€)** 🚆 **RENFE Benalmádena Arroyo de la Miel** ♿ **Few** 💵 **Moderate**

Benalmádena Costa
Sea Life
A submarine view of Mediterranean sea life from tiny shrimps and shellfish to sharks. There are various organised presentations and the feeding displays are always popular.

✉ **Puerto Marina, Benalmádena** ☎ **952 56 01 50** 🕐 **Daily 10–6 & Restaurants (€€)** 🚆 **RENFE Benalmádena** ♿ **Good** 💵 **Moderate**

Estepona
Selwo Aventura
A magnificent wild animal park covering 100ha where you can see such animals as lions and elephants in their natural habitat.

✉ **Autovía Costa del Sol, Km 162.5, Las Lomas del Monte** ☎ **952 79 21 50** 🕐 **Mon–Fri 10–6, Sun 10–7:30** ♿ **Few** 💵 **Moderate**

Fuengirola
Zoo Fuengirola
Magnificent new zoo where numerous species of animals and birds can be seen in their natural habitat.

✉ **Camilo José Cela** ☎ **952 66 63 01** 🕐 **Daily 10–6** 💵 **Moderate**

Mijas Costa
Parque Acuático Mijas

Very wet. A big water fun park with endless pools, slides and flumes. Also on site is 'Aqualandia', a water play area for small children. Also mini-golf and self-service cafeteria, deposit boxes for valuables, and picnic area. Sunbeds, air mattresses and floats for hire. For obvious reasons, there is a strict warning not to bring any form of glass object into the park.

✉ **Circunvalación, Km 290** ☎ **952 46 04 04/08/09; fax 952 46 94 42** 🕐 **May, daily 10:30–5:30; Jun 10–6; Jul–Aug 10–7; Sep–Oct 3 10–6. Cafeteria (€€)** 🚌 **Direct from Fuengirola bus terminal** ♿ **Few** 💵 **Expensive**

Torremolinos
Aquapark
A major site with scores of popular water-based attractions including huge slides, flumes, artificial river, artificial waves, pools, jacuzzi and much more.

✉ **c/ Cuba 10** ☎ **952 11 49 96/38 88 88; fax 952 37 01 99** 🕐 **May–Oct daily, 10–late, inc. Café/ restaurant (€€)** 🚌 **Direct service from Benalmadena Costa Jul–Aug** ♿ **Few** 💵 **Expensive**

Crocodile Park
'Monstrous prehistoric monsters' is how this unique attraction is described in its publicity. There are crocodiles large and small to keep everyone amazed. Watch them being fed, at a safe distance. Handle cuddly baby alligators, and visit the 'Africa' museum.

✉ **Calle Cuba 14** ☎ **952 05 17 82** 🕐 **Mar–Jun, Oct, Nov 10–6; Jul–Sep 10–5** ♿ **Poor** 💵 **Moderate**

Safety First
Spain is a country where children are revered, but attitudes to what is safe and not safe may differ from your own. You will see very young children being whizzed around sitting on the petrol tank in front of a youthful motorcyclist . The fact that a black-clad grandmother is often whooping it up on the pillion without a crash helmet in sight says it all. This is exuberance, not carelessness. When you have seen bull-running at places like Arcos de la Frontera, where young teenagers leap and dance in front of the bulls, you will appreciate this very different idea of what constitutes risk.

Take care of children where there is a lot of city traffic. Impatient scooter drivers often bump up on to the pavement to get round traffic jams. Watch out for unguarded holes in pavements, especially as the light fades. Think carefully about what level of sun protection is needed for youngsters, as well as yourselves. Very young children should be covered up, without discomfort, to protect them from the often searing Andalucían sun.

Nightlife and Flamenco

Flamenco

Flamenco is one of the enduring symbols of Andalucía. The frilly, brilliantly coloured dresses, the *batas de cola* worn by female dancers, the passionate intensity of singers, the rhythmic hand-clapping *jaleo*, the *staccato* footwork and sinuous movements of good dancers, all combine to produce one of the world's most exhilarating dance spectacles. It is hard to avoid this flamenco 'experience' in Andalucía, though it may not always be authentic. Experts will tell you, loftily, that the real thing erupts spontaneously, and only after midnight, in neighbourhood bars and in semiprivate *juergas* or all-night '*binges*'. You may have to settle for a set piece 'flamenco evening' booked through hotels and tour operators. For performances of 'classical' flamenco by trained artistes, ask at Tourism Offices.

Almería

Georgia Café Bar

Long-standing favourite. Good ambience. Live jazz on occasion.

✉ **Calle Padre Luque 17**
☎ **950 25 70 ??**

Cadiz

El Malecón

One of the most popular spots for Latin-style dancing.

✉ **Paseo Pascual Pery**
☎ **956 22 45 19**

Córdoba

La Toscana

Club with large outside terrace for dancing.

✉ **Ctra de Trassierra km3**

Granada

El Camborio

Swinging dance club with a young ambience. Very busy at weekends.

✉ **Camino del Sacremonte**
☎ **No phone**

Seville

Fun Club

With all types of music, ranging from Latin American to jazz. Live bands at the weekend. A great place for dance enthusiasts.

✉ **Alameda de Hércules 86**
☎ **650 48 98 58**

La Imperdible

Excellent café-bar with a whole range of live music, from jazz to flamenco. Action really gets under way about 10PM. Closed Monday.

✉ **Plaza San Antonio de Padua 9** ☎ **954 38 82 19**

Costa del Sol

Benalmádena Costa

Casino Torrequebrada/ Fortuna Night Club

The place to come for Black Jack, roulette, poker, slot machines and a glitzy floor show. Passports must be shown at reception.

✉ **Avenida del Sol** ☎ **952 44 60 00; fax 952 44 57 02** 🕐 **Daily 8PM–4AM**

Tivoli World

There is a full range of musical entertainment here including flamenco, country and western and popular musicals.

✉ **Arroyo de la Miel**
☎ **952 57 70 16**

Fuengirola

Moochers Jazz Café

Live music and giant pancakes are on offer iin this popular jazz and Hollywood themed bar-restaurant.

✉ **c/de la Cruz 17**
☎ **952 47 71 54**

Málaga

O'Neill's Irish Pub

Popular for draught Guinness and big doses of Irish music.

✉ **c/Luis del Velazquez 3**
☎ **952 60 14 60**

Marbella

Casino Marbella

Blackjack, roulette, poker and slot machines. Passports must be shown at reception.

✉ **Bajos del Hotel, Andalucía Plaza** ☎ **952 81 40 00; fax 952 81 28 44** 🕐 **Slot machines 4PM–early hours. Casino 8PM–early hours. Restaurant 9PM–3AM**

Oliviere Valeres

Late night venue decorated in mock Moorish style. Huge dance floor and a variety of bars. Terrace for cooling off between sessions.

✉ **Istan road** ☎ **952 82 88 61**
🕐 **Daily 8PM–4AM**

Flamenco

Flamenco takes many forms and is besieged with secrets and subtleties. The visitor will have difficulty in identifying the completely authentic venue or catching the ultimate *flamenco puro* in all its spontaneous glory. There are countless venues offering flamenco performances and these range from big set-piece shows in restaurants and theatres to suspect bars and 'gypsy caves'. Unless advised by a genuine aficionado and accompanied by such to an authentic venue, it is probably best to experience flamenco through established shows recommended by tourist information offices or hotels.

Baeza
Peña Flamenco
Occasional flamenco performances are staged here. Detials from the tourist information office.
✉ Conde Romanones 6

Córdoba
Tablao Cardenal
One of the best venues for 'classical' flamenco. Performances are staged in a delightful patio with an authentic ambience, right opposite the Mezquita. Bar and restaurant service. Reservations advised.
✉ c/ Torrijos 10 ☎ 957 48 33 20; fax 957 48 31 12

Granada
Los Tarantos
Touristy but fun flamenco show in the atmospheric setting of the caves of Sacramonte
✉ Camino del Sacramento 9
☎ 958 22 45 25 (day), 958 22 24 92 (night) ◷ Fri and Sat

Jerez de la Frontera
Fundación Andaluza de Flamenco
Jerez is one of the great centres of flamenco and the Fundación performances are authentic 'classical' flamenco at its best.
✉ Plaza San Juan 1
☎ 956 34 92 65

Málaga
Teatro Miguel de Cervantes
Regular flamenco shows are staged at this theatre and are of a good standard.
✉ Ramos Marín s/n
☎ 952 22 41 00

Seville
El Arenal
A very lavish flamenco theatre and restaurant with stage shows, with or without meal. This is very much set-piece flamenco, but is well done and enjoyable. It caters mainly for coach parties, but individual reservations can be made ,and you are advised to book if you want to go alone.
✉ c/ Rodo 7 ☎ 954 21 64 92
◷ Daily 9PM, 11:30PM

Los Gallos
Although this is a smaller venue than El Arenal, it still has a good and lively atmosphere.
✉ Plaza de Santa Cruz
☎ 954 21 69 81
◷ Daily. 9PM, 11:30PM

Úbeda
Peña Flamenco El Quejío
This flamenco venue stages occasional shows that really are worth attending. Ask at the tourist information centre for details and times of shows.
✉ Alfareros 4

Bullfighting

The *corrida de toros*, the bullfight, defines Spain as intensely as flamenco does. Both are viewed as art forms by the Spanish; both exhibit passion, pain and balletic elegance. Flamenco does not, however, involve the protracted torment and death of an animal, and it is this which defines bullfighting for most visitors as unequivocally cruel. The last thing you may want to see on holiday is a *corrida*, but it may be forced upon you, at one remove at least, on the television screens of countless bars, where it is watched by Andalucíans more intently at times than football. The bullfighting season runs from April to October and even some of the smallest villages stage *corridas* during their annual festivals. Larger towns and main cities all have a programme of regular *corridas* that are prominently advertised.

Sports & Activities

Horses

Horses and horse-riding have a special appeal in Andalucía, the home of world-class horsemanship and open spaces. If you attend a big fiesta you will be sure to see horses and riders in all their finery. In remote villages the ubiquitous presence of motorbike and scooter is often eclipsed, however momentarily, by the more melodious clatter of horses' hooves, as young riders from surrounding farms pass through, dusty from field and track. Throughout Andalucía there are a number of riding schools that organise leisure rides and also give lessons in basic dressage and jumping skills. In the mountain areas, horse-trekking is a delightful way of seeing the Andalucían countryside.

Equestrian

Jerez

Real Escuela Andaluze del Arte Ecuestre (Royal Andalucían School of Equestrian Art)

An unmissable experience. Even if horses are not your passion, they will become so during this superb display. Enjoy breathtaking equestrian movements in the Royal School's handsome arena.

✉ Avda Duque de Abrantes ☎ 956 31 96 35/00; fax 956 18 07 57 🕐 Mar –Oct Tue, Thu noon; Mar–Oct Mon, Wed, Fri 11, 1. Tours of stables and training sessions 🎫 Expensive

Él Burgo

Ride in the beautiful Sierra Nevada to the east of Ronda, while based at a country inn.

✉ Posada del Canoigo ☎ 952 16 01 85

Parque Natural de Doñana

Doñana Ecuestre
Day-long rides through marshland.

✉ El Rocío ☎ 959 44 24 74

Costa del Sol

Estepona

Escuela de Arte Ecuestre 'Costa del Sol'
Riding centre where you learn about the skills required to handle these famous Andalucían horses. Weekly dressage displays – Fridays in summer and Tuesdays in winter.

✉ Cn. 340, Km 159, Río Padrón Alto s/n ☎ 959 44 24 66

Torremolinos

Hípica International
Half day rides available for experienced riders. Jumping and dressage lessons.

✉ Camino de la Sierra ☎ 952 43 55 49

Bird Watching

Parque Nacional Coto de Doñana

The Coto de Doñana National Park has a wealth of resident wildlife and migratory birds, the latter especially in spring and autumn. 4-wheel drive tours available at visitor centre. Bird watching trips are organised by Discovering Donaña, tel 959 44 24 66.

✉ Doñana Visitor Centre ☎ 959 44 23 40; jeep tour reservations 959 43 04 32

Golf

Golfing visitors to Andalucía will find plenty of opportunities for their sport.

Benalmádena

Golf Torrequebrada
18 holes, par 72. Moderate fee.

✉ Ctra de Cádiz, N340 ☎ 952 44 27 42

Estepona

Estepona Golf
18 holes, par 72. Reasonable fee.

✉ Apartado 532 ☎ 952 11 30 81

Málaga

Alhaurin Golf & Country Club
45 holes, par 72. Reasonable green fee.

✉ Mijas-Alhaurín el Grande ☎ 952 59 59 70

Marbella

Golf Club Marbella
18 holes, par 71. Expensive.

✉ Ctra de Cádiz ☎ 952 83 05 00

La Quinta Golf & Country Club
27 holes, par 72. Moderate fee.
✉ Ctra. de Ronda, Km 3.5
☎ 952 76 23 90

Hang-gliding and Paragliding

In the Valle de Abdalajís, near Málaga, thermal conditions are especially good for hang-gliding and paragliding.

Club Escuela de Parapente Abdalajís
✉ Valle de Abdalajís s/n
☎ 952 48 91 80

Club Vuelo Libre Málaga
Week-long beginners courses available. Also two-seater flights with instructor. Accommodation available.
✉ Valle de Abdalajís s/n
☎ 952 48 92 98

Hot-air ballooning

Aviación del Sol
Club Vuelo Libre Málaga
Organises hot air balloon trips over land and sea.
✉ Aptdo 344, Ronda
☎ 952 87 72 49

Adventure Sports

Grazalema
Horizon
For the fit and the adventurous, Horizon offers a whole range of outdoor activities including caving, rock-climbing, mountain-biking, paragliding and trekking, in the spectacular Sierra de Grazalema's Parque Natural.
✉ c/Agua 5 ☎ 956 13 23 63; fax 956 13 23 63

Sierra Cazorla
A whole range of activities is available throughout the region – trekking, camping, mountain-biking, canoeing, horse-riding – all in the magnificent setting of the Sierra Cazorla Parque

Natural. For information, contact Agencia de Medio Ambiente (AMA), Tejares Altos, Cazorla (tel 953 72 01 25) or the Centro de Interpretación Torre del Vinagre located 16km northeast of Emplame de Valle (tel 953 71 30 40).

Water Sports

Almuñécar
Buceo La Herradura
Diving courses available from 1- to 4-day programmes.
✉ Marine del Este ☎ 958 82 70 83

Cabo De Gata
Puerto Deportivo de San José
Diving in the protected Cabo de Gata Nature Park.
✉ San José ☎ 950 38 00 41

Benalmádena Puerta Deportivo
Club Nautico Diving Centre
Diving courses available all year at the Marina.
✉ Puerta Marina, Benalmádena s/n
☎ 952 56 07 69

Istán
Tickets-to-Ride
20 minutes from Marbella, individual and group canoeing trips.
✉ Istán Lake ☎ 609 51 75 17

Windsurfing
The Costa del Luz is noted for its excellent wind-surfing conditions, especially in its southern section.

Cádiz
Centro Naútico Elcano
✉ Prolongacion de Ronda de Vigilancia s/n ☎ 956 26 58 00; fax 956 26 49 89

Tarifa
Club Mistral
✉ Hurricane Hotel
☎ 956 68 90 98

Tourist Information Offices
When looking for information on entertainment, events and other matters, you may find that the service at tourist information offices in main cities can be variable. At the big offices, staff who have to deal with a constant stream of enquiries sometimes seem to suffer from understandable 'enquiry fatigue'. In some rural towns and villages you may meet with apparent indifference. If you do not speak much Spanish, this, too, is understandable: many provincial tourism offices are used to dealing with mainly Spanish tourists. In other rural information offices you will be greeted by efficient and enthusiastic service. In very remote areas and isolated villages, the Ayuntamiento (Town Hall) is often the only source of information. At most town halls, you will be treated with kindness and, even in the absence of a shared language, people will do their best to help.

What's On When

Pride & Passion

The *festival* (festival), the *feria* (fair) and the *fiesta* (holiday) are at the heart of Andalucían culture. The *festival* is often religious in its elements. The *feria* originates from livestock fairs and today is significant for much flamboyant horsemanship; *romerías* are religious processions culminating in a picnic. The line between the religious and the secular is blurred in Andalucía, and the same earthy passion is expressed during the most intense religious periods such as Holy Week as at the life-affirming spring celebrations. Celebration is so inherent to life in Andalucía that visitors are likely to find themselves with some form of local *feria* or *festival* due in their locality. Do not miss out on them if you want to get near to the absolute, exuberant, passionate essence of Andalucía.

January

6 Jan: *Cabalgata de los Reyes Magos*, Málaga. Epiphany parade.

February

Pre-Lenten, week-long *Carnaval* in many Andalucían towns and cities, including Antequera, Cádiz, Carmona, Córdoba, Málaga: mid-month.

March/April

Semana Santa, Holy Week. Follows Palm Sun and is one of the most powerful and passionate celebrations in the world. Most colourful and dramatic in Seville.

April

Month of the most exuberant *ferias*, that of Seville being considered the best and biggest in Spain. Held one or two weeks after Easter, but always in April. Vejer de la Frontera holds an Easter Sun *feria*, with bull-running through the streets.

May

First week: Horse Fair, Jerez de la Frontera.
Fiesta de las Patios. Córdoba's fabulous private patios are open to the public in early May.
Romería del Rocío. Whitsun. Vast numbers congregate at the village of El Rocío, Huelva, to celebrate the *La Blanca Paloma*, the 'White Dove', the Virgen del Rocío.
Corpus Christi. Thursday after Trinity Sun. Festivals and bullfights; Seville, Granada, Ronda, Zahara de la Sierra, and at smaller towns and villages.

June

Second week: *Feria de San Barnabé*. Marbella.

13–14 June: *San Antonio Fiesta*. Trevélez, Las Alpujarras. Mock battles between Moors and Christians.

July

La Virgen del Carmen. Fuengirola, Estepona, Marbella Nerja, and Torremolinos. Celebrates the patron saint of fishermen.

August

5 Aug: *Mulhacén Romería*, Trevélez. Midnight procession to Sierra Nevada's highest peak.
13–21 Aug: *Feria de Málaga*. Very lively fiesta.
Mid-Aug: *horse-racing*; Sanlúcar de Barrameda. Races along the sandy beaches.
Third weekend: *Fiesta de San Mames*, Aroche. Friendly village fiesta.

September

7 Sep: *Romería del Cristo de la Yedra*, Baeza. Street processions and entertainment.
6–13 Sep: *Festival Virgen de la Luz*, Tarifa.
First two weeks: *Pedro Romero Fiestas*, Ronda. Celebration of famous bullfighter.

October

15–23 Oct: *Feria de San Lucas*, Jaén. The city's main festival.
6–12 Oct: *Feria del Rosario*, Fuengirola. Horse riding and flamenco.

December

28 Dec: *Fiesta de los Verdiales*, Malaga province. Lively, theatrical and musical event in villages to the north of Málaga.

Practical Matters

Above: *one of Seville's colourful and smart buses*
Right: *'Danger of Fire' warning sign in the vulnerable mountains of Andalucía*

TIME DIFFERENCES

GMT	Spain	Germany	USA (NY)	Netherlands
12 noon	→ 1PM	→ 1PM	← 7AM	→ 1PM

BEFORE YOU GO

WHAT YOU NEED

- ● Required
- ○ Suggested
- ▲ Not required

Some countries require a passport to remain valid for a minimum period (usually at least six months) beyond the date of entry – contact their consulate or embassy or your travel agent for details.

	UK	Germany	USA	Netherlands
Passport/National Identity Card	●	●	●	●
Visa (regulations can change – check before your journey)	▲	▲	▲	▲
Onward or Return Ticket	▲	▲	●	●
Health Inoculations	▲	▲	▲	▲
Health Documentation (reciprocal agreement document) (► 123, Health)	●	●	▲	●
Travel Insurance	○	○	○	○
Driving Licence (national – EU format/national/Spanish trnsltn/interntnal)	●	●	●	●
Car Insurance Certificate (if own car)	●	●	●	●
Car Registration Document (if own car)	●	●	●	●

WHEN TO GO

Average figures for Andalucía

High season

Low season

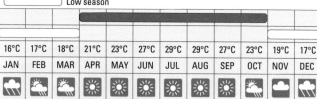

JAN	FEB	MAR	APR	MAY	JUN	JUL	AUG	SEP	OCT	NOV	DEC
16°C	17°C	18°C	21°C	23°C	27°C	29°C	29°C	27°C	23°C	19°C	17°C

 Wet   Cloud   Sun   Sunshine & showers

TOURIST OFFICES

In the UK
Spanish Tourist Office,
79 New Cavendish Street,
London W1W 6XB
☎ 020 7486 8077
Fax: 020 7486 8034
www.spain.info
www.andalucia.com

In the USA
Tourist Office of Spain,
35th Floor, 665 Fifth Ave
New York, NY 10103
☎ 212 265 8822
Fax: 212 265 8864

Tourist Office of Spain
8383 Wilshire Boulevard
Suite 960
Beverley Hills, CA 90211
☎ 213 658 7192
Fax: 213 658 1061

POLICE (Policía Nacional) 091; (Policía Local) 092

AMBULANCE (Ambulancia) 061

FIRE (Bomberos) 080

WHEN YOU ARE THERE

ARRIVING

Almería Airport
Kilometres to city centre

8 kilometres

Journey times

🚕 25 minutes

🚌 20 minutes

Málaga Airport
Kilometres to city centre

10 kilometres

Journey times

🚕 12 minutes

🚌 20 minutes

🚆 20 minutes

Seville Airport
Kilometres to city centre

8 kilometres

Journey times

🚕 N/A

🚌 20 minutes

🚆 20 minutes

MONEY

Spain's currency is the euro which is divided into 100 cents. Coins come in denominations of 1, 2, 5, 10, 20 and 50 cents, 1 and 2 euros, and notes come in 5, 10, 20, 50, 100, 200 and 500 euro denominations (the last two are rarely seen). The notes and one side of the coins are the same throughout the European single currency zone. Notes and coins from any of the other countries can be used in Spain.

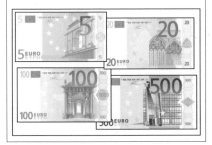

TIME

 Spain is one hour ahead of Greenwich Mean Time (GMT+1), but from late March until the last Sunday in October, summer time (GMT+2) operates.

CUSTOMS

 YES
From another EU country for personal use (guidelines):
800 cigarettes, 200 cigars, 1 kilogram of tobacco
10 litres of spirits (over 22%)
20 litres of aperitifs
90 litres of wine, of which 60 litres can be sparkling wine
110 litres of beer

From a non-EU country for your personal use, the allowances are:
200 cigarettes OR
50 cigars OR 250 grams of tobacco
1 litre of spirits (over 22%)
2 litres of intermediary products (e.g. sherry) and sparkling wine
2 litres of still wine
50 grams of perfume
0.25 litres of eau de toilette
The value limit for goods is 175 euros.

Travellers under 17 years of age are not entitled to the tobacco and alcohol allowances.

 NO
Drugs, firearms, ammunition, offensive weapons, obscene material, unlicensed animals.

CONSULATES

UK
952 21 75 71
(Málaga)

Germany
952 21 24 42
(Málaga)

USA
952 47 48 91
(Fuengirola)

Netherlands
952 27 99 54
(Málaga)

WHEN YOU ARE THERE

TOURIST OFFICES

Almería
- Parque Nicolás Salmerón s/n
  ☎ 950 27 43 55

- Baeza
  Plaza del Pópulo s/n
  ☎ and fax 953 74 04 44

- Cádiz
  Avenida Ramón de Carranza s/n
  ☎ 956 25 86 46

- Córdoba
  Calle Torrijos 10
  ☎ 957 47 12 35

- Granada
  Corral del Carbón,
  c/ Libreras 2,
  ☎ 958 22 59 90
  Municipal Tourist Office,
  Plaza Mariana Pineda 10
  ☎ 958 24 71 28

- Huelva
  Avda de Alemania 12
  ☎ 959 25 74 03

- Jaén
  Maestra 13
  ☎ 953 24 26 24

- Málaga
  Pasaje de Chinitas 4
  ☎ 952 21 34 45
  Aeropuerto Internacional
  (Airport) ☎ 952 04 84 84
  (ext. 58617)

- Ronda
  Plaza de España 1
  ☎ and fax 952 87 12 72

- Seville
  Avda de Kansas City s/n,
  Estación de Santa Justa
  ☎ 954 53 76 26
  Aeropuerto de San Pablo
  (airport) ☎ 954 44 91 28

- Úbeda
  Bajo de Marqués 4
  ☎ 954 75 08 97

NATIONAL HOLIDAYS

J	F	M	A	M	J	J	A	S	O	N	D
2	1	1	1	1	1	1	1			1	1	3

1 Jan	New Year's Day
6 Jan	Epiphany
28 Feb	Andalucían Day (regional)
Mar/Apr	Maundy Thursday, Good Friday, Easter Monday
1 May	Labour Day
24 Jun	San Juan (regional)
25 Jul	Santiago (regional)
15 Aug	Assumption of the Virgin
12 Oct	National Day
1 Nov	All Saints' Day
6 Dec	Constitution Day
8 Dec	Feast of the Immaculate Conception
25 Dec	Christmas Day

OPENING HOURS

○ Shops   ● Pharmacies
● Offices   ◐ Museums/Monuments
● Banks   ○ Churches

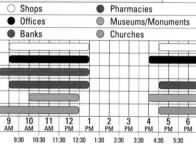

In addition to the times shown above, department stores, large supermarkets and shops in tourist resorts open from 10AM through to 8, 9 or even 10PM. The vast majority of shops close Sun and some close in Aug. Most banks open 9–2 Monday to Friday, some banks open 9–2 Saturday. The opening times of museums is just a rough guide; some open longer in summer, while hours may be reduced in winter. Many museums close Sun afternoon, some also on Sat afternoon, as well as Mon or another day in the week. Some museums offer free entry to EU citizens (take your passport). **Remember – all opening times are subject to change.**

**DRIVE ON THE
RIGHT**

**TOILETS
FREE**

PUBLIC TRANSPORT

Internal Flights
The national airline, Iberia, plus the smaller Aviaco, operate an extensive network of internal flights. Iberia Airline Offices; Granada ☎ 958 22 75 92; Málaga ☎ 952 13 61 47; Sevilla ☎ 954 98 82 08. For reservations on domestic flights ☎ 902 40 05 00. Not cheap but worth considering if in a hurry.

Trains
Services are provided by the state-run company – RENFE. Fares are among the cheapest in Europe. For rail inquiries call Almería ☎ 950 23 18 22; Cádiz ☎ 902 24 02 02; Córdoba ☎ 957 40 02 02/902 24 02 02; Granada ☎ 902 24 02 02/958 20 40 00; Seville ☎ 954 54 02 02/902 24 02 02 Málaga ☎ 952 36 02 02/902 24 02 02

Buses
There is a comprehensive and reliable bus network operated by different companies along the coast and to inland towns and villages. Fares are very reasonable. Go to the local bus station for details of routes. Almería ☎ 950 26 20 98; Cádiz ☎ 956 28 58 52/956 21 17 63; Córdoba ☎ 957 40 40 40; Granada ☎ 958 18 54 80/98; Seville ☎ 954 41 71 11 Málaga ☎ 952 35 00 61.

Urban Transport
Traffic in the cities of Andalucía generally and in the main towns and resorts of the Costa del Sol in particular, is normally heavy, especially in summer, but public transport in the form of buses is generally good.

CAR RENTAL

The leading international car rental companies operate in the main cities and on the Costa del Sol. You can hire a car in advance (essential at peak periods) either direct or through a travel agent. Hiring from a local firm can work out cheaper.

TAXIS

Only use taxis which display a licence issued by the local authority. Taxis show a green light when available for hire. They can be flagged down in the street. In cities and large towns taxis are metered; where they are not, determine the price of the journey in advance.

DRIVING

Speed limits on *autopistas* (toll motorways) and *autovías* (free motorways): **120kph**; dual carriageways and roads with overtaking lanes: **100kph**. Take care on the N340 coastal highway as this is a particularly dangerous road.

Speed limits on country roads: **90kph**

Speed limits on urban roads: **50kph**; in residential areas: **20kph**

Must be worn in front seats at all times and in rear seats where fitted.

Random breath-testing. Never drive under the influence of alcohol.

Fuel (*gasolina*) is available in four grades: *Normal* (92 octane); *Super* (98 octane); *Sin plomo* (unleaded, 95 and 98 octane); and *gasoleo* or *gasoil* (diesel). Petrol prices are fixed by the Government and are lower than those in the UK. Most

If you break down with your own car and are a member of an AIT-affiliated motoring club, call the Real Automóvil Club de España, or RACE (☎ 915 94 74 00) for assistance. If the car is hired you should follow the instructions in the documentation; most international rental firms provide a rescue service.

Above the main content is a ruler graphic showing CENTIMETRES (0–8) and INCHES (0–3).

PERSONAL SAFETY

Snatching of handbags and cameras, pick-pocketing, theft of unattended baggage and car break-ins are the principal crimes against visitors. Any crime or loss should be reported to the national police force (*Policía Nacional*) who wear blue uniforms. Some precautions:

- Do not leave valuables on the beach or poolside
- Place valuables in a hotel safety-deposit box
- Wear handbags and cameras across your chest
- Avoid lonely, seedy and dark areas at night

Police assistance:
☎ **091**
from any call box

ELECTRICITY

The power supply is: 220/230 volts (in some bathrooms and older buildings: 110/120 volts).

 Type of socket: round two-hole sockets taking round plugs of two round pins. British visitors will need an adaptor and US visitors a voltage transformer.

TELEPHONES

All telephone numbers throughout Spain now consist of nine digits and you must always dial all nine digits. Local calls are inexpensive. Although you can pay with coins, it is quicker and easier to

 buy a phonecard from any *tabaco* (tobacconist). Many phones also take credit cards. Long-distance calls are cheaper from a booth than from your hotel. Directory information is 003.

International Dialling Codes

From Spain to:	
UK:	00 44
Germany:	00 49
USA:	00 1
Netherlands:	00 31

POST

Post Offices
Post offices (*correos*) are generally open as below; in main centres they may open extended hours. Málaga's main post office is at Avenida de Andalucía 1. Stamps (*sellos*) can also be bought at tobacconists (*estancos*).
Open: 9–2 (1PM Sat)
Closed: Sun
☎ 902 29 72 97 (Málaga)

TIPS/GRATUITIES

Yes ✓ No ✗		
Restaurants (if service not included)	✓	5–10%
Cafés/bars	✓	change
Taxis	✓	2–3%
Tour Guides	✓	change
Porters	✓	change
Chambermaids	✓	change
Hairdressers	✓	change
Cloakroom attendants	✓	change
Theatre/cinema usherettes	✓	change
Toilets	✓	change

PHOTOGRAPHY
What to photograph: the rugged coast, unspoilt inland villages, examples of Moorish architecture, and panoramas of the Sierra Nevada.
Best times to photograph: the summer sun can be too bright at the height of the day making photos taken at this time appear 'flat'. It is best to take photographs in the early morning or late evening.
Where to buy film: film (*rollo/carrete*) and camera batteries (*pilas*) are readily available from tourist shops, department stores and photo shops.

HEALTH

Insurance
EU nationals can get some free medical treatment with the relevant documentation (Form E111 for Britons), although medical insurance is still advised and is essential for all other visitors. US visitors should check their insurance coverage.

Dental Services
Dental treatment normally has to be paid for in full as dentists operate privately. A list of *dentistas* can be found in the yellow pages of the telephone directory. Dental treatment should be covered by private medical insurance.

Sun Advice
The sunniest (and hottest) months are July and August when daytime temperatures are often into the 30°s C. Try to avoid the midday sun and use a high-factor sun cream to start with, and allow yourself to become used to the sun gradually.

Drugs
Prescriptions and non-prescription drugs and medicines are available from pharmacies (*farmácias*), distinguished by a large green cross. They are able to dispense many drugs which are available only on prescription in other countries.

Safe Water
Tap water is chlorinated and generally safe to drink; however, unfamiliar water may cause mild abdominal upsets. Mineral water (*agua mineral*) is cheap and widely available. It is sold *sin gas* (still) and *con gas* (carbonated).

CONCESSIONS

Students/Youths Holders of an International Student Identity Card (ISIC) may be able to obtain some concessions on travel, entrance fees etc, but the Costa del Sol is not really geared up for students (special facilities and programmes are limited). The main advantage for students and young people is that low-cost package deals are available.

Senior Citizens The Costa del Sol is an excellent destination for older travellers – travel agents offer tailored package holidays. In winter there are special low-cost, long-stay holidays for senior citizens; the best deals are available through tour operators who specialise in holidays for senior citizens.

CLOTHING SIZES

Spain	UK	Rest of Europe	USA	
46	36	46	36	
48	38	48	38	
50	40	50	40	
52	42	52	42	Suits
54	44	54	44	
56	46	56	46	
41	7	41	8	
42	7.5	42	8.5	
43	8.5	43	9.5	
44	9.5	44	10.5	Shoes
45	10.5	45	11.5	
46	11	46	12	
37	14.5	37	14.5	
38	15	38	15	
39/40	15.5	39/40	15.5	
41	16	41	16	Shirts
42	16.5	42	16.5	
43	17	43	17	
34	8	34	6	
36	10	36	8	
38	12	38	10	
40	14	40	12	Dresses
42	16	42	14	
44	18	44	16	
38	4.5	38	6	
38	5	38	6.5	
39	5.5	39	7	
39	6	39	7.5	Shoes
40	6.5	40	8	
41	7	41	8.5	

WHEN DEPARTING

- Remember to contact the airport or airline on the day prior to leaving to ensure that the flight details are unchanged.

- There is no airport departure tax to pay so you can happily spend your last remaining euros.

- Spanish customs are usually polite and normally easy to negotiate.

LANGUAGE

Spanish is one of the easiest languages. All vowels are pure and short (as in English). Some useful tips on speaking: 'c' is lisped before 'e' and 'i', otherwise hard; 'h' is silent; 'j' is pronounced like a gutteral 'j'; 'r' is rolled; 'v' sounds more like 'b'; and 'z' is the same as a soft 'c'. English is widely spoken in the principal resorts but you will get a better reception if you at least try communicating with Spaniards in their own tongue. More extensive coverage can be found in the AA's *Essential Spanish Phrase Book* which lists over 2,000 phrases and 2,000 words.

hotel	*hotel*	breakfast	*desayuno*
room	*habitación*	toilet	*lavabo*
single/double	*individual/doble*	bath	*baño*
one/two nights	*una/dos noche(s)*	shower	*ducha*
per person/per room	*por persona/por habitación*	en suite	*en su habitación*
		balcony	*balcón*
reservation	*reserva*	key	*llave*
rate	*precio*	chambermaid	*camarera*

bank	*banco*	American dollar	*dólar estadounidense*
exchange office	*oficina de cambio*		
post office	*correos*	bank card	*tarjeta del banco*
cashier	*cajero*	credit card	*tarjeta de crédito*
money	*dinero*	giro bank card	*tarjeta de la caja postal*
coin	*moneda*		
foreign currency	*moneda extranjera*	cheque	*cheque*
change money	*cambiar dinero*	traveller's cheque	*cheque de viajero*
pound sterling	*libra esterlina*	giro cheque	*cheque postal*

restaurant	*restaurante*	snack	*merienda*
bar	*bar*	starter	*primer plato*
table	*mesa*	dish	*plato*
menu	*carta*	main course	*plato principal*
tourist menu	*menú turístico*	dessert	*postre*
wine list	*carta de vinos*	drink	*bebida*
lunch	*almuerzo*	waiter	*camarero*
dinner	*cena*	bill	*cuenta*

aeroplane	*avión*	ferry	*transbordador*
airport	*aeropuerto*	port	*puerto*
flight	*vuelo*	ticket	*billete*
train	*tren*	single/return	*ida/ida y vuelta*
station	*estación ferrocarril*	first/second class	*primera/segunda clase*
bus	*autobús*		
station	*estación de autobuses*	timetable	*horario*
		seat	*asiento*
stop	*parada de autobús*	non-smoking	*no fumadores*

yes	*sí*	help!	*ayuda!*
no	*no*	today	*hoy*
please	*por favór*	tomorrow	*mañana*
thank you	*gracias*	yesterday	*ayer*
hello	*hola*	how much?	*cuánto?*
goodbye	*adiós*	expensive	*caro*
good night	*buenas noches*	open	*abierto*
excuse me	*perdóneme*	closed	*cerrado*

Acknowledgements

The Automobile Association would like to thank the following photographers and libraries for the assistance in the preparation of this book.

ANDALUCIA SLIDE LIBRARY 5b, 7b, 8b, 8c, 9b, 9c, 17a, 18b, 42, 44b, 51a52b, 53b, 55, 56c, 57, 63b, 66b, 67a, 70a, 70b, 73b, 77, 78, 80, 81a, 82a, 83a, 84a, 86a, 86b, 86c, 87b, 88a, 89b, 90a, 90b, 91a, 92, 93, 94, 95, 96, 97, 98, 99, 100, 101, 102, 103, 104, 105, 106, 107, 108, 109, 110, 111, 112, 113, 114, 115, 116, 122a, 122b; DES HANNIGAN 35b, 38b, 49b, 50b, 74b, 83b; HULTON GETTY 11a, 14b, 14c; REX FEATURES 11b; WORLD PICTURES 54b; www.euro.ecb.int 119 (euro notes).

The remaining pictures are held in the associations own library (AA PHOTOLIBRARY) and were taken by Michelle Chaplow, with the exception of Peter Baker 122c; J Edmanson 13c, 16b, 17b, 21b, 24c, 27a, 28, 29, 33c, 34b, 45c, 69b, 82b; Andrew Molyneux 2, 10b, 15b, 76, 79a, 117a; J Paulson 65b, 72b; Douglas Roberson 5a, 6a, 7a, 8a, 9a, 10a, 12a, 12b, 13a, 14a, 33b, 40b, 43, 44a, 45a, 45b, 46a, 47, 48a, 49a, 50a, 51b, 52a, 53a, 54a, 56a, 58a, 67b, 68b, 84b, 89a, 117b; James Tims F/cover (a) bullfighter, 60, 61, 62a, 63a, 64a, 64b, 65a, 66a, 68a, 69a, 71b, 72a, 74a, 75a; Peter Wilson F/cover (e) cathedral dome, (f) bodegas barrel, (g) local fiesta, (h) church tower, (i) boat, bottom tiles, B/cover riding school

Author's Acknowledgements

Des Hannigan thanks the very helpful staffs of Almería Turismo and of the municipal Turismos in Cádiz and Granada. Special thanks to Cele Cuesta of Montefrío and Paula Moreno Robledo of Carmona. Thanks also for good company and advice to Ana Griffin, Pam and Rob Murray, Lewis Richards and Sharon Stokes, and to countless Andalucían friends and acquaintances along the way.

Dear Essential Traveller

Your comments, opinions and recommendations are very important to us. So please help us to improve our travel guides by taking a few minutes to complete this simple questionnaire.

You do not need a stamp (unless posted outside the UK). If you do not want to cut this page from your guide, then photocopy it or write your answers on a plain sheet of paper.

Send to: **The Editor, AA World Travel Guides, FREEPOST SCE 4598, Basingstoke RG21 4GY.**

Your recommendations...

We always encourage readers' recommendations for restaurants, nightlife or shopping – if your recommendation is used in the next edition of the guide, we will send you a ***FREE* AA *Essential* Guide** of your choice. Please state below the establishment name, location and your reasons for recommending it.

_____

_____

_____

_____

Please send me **AA *Essential*** _____

About this guide...

Which title did you buy?

AA *Essential* _____

Where did you buy it? _____

When? m m / y y

Why did you choose an AA *Essential* Guide? _____

_____

_____

_____

_____

Did this guide meet your expectations?

Exceeded ☐ Met all ☐ Met most ☐ Fell below ☐

Please give your reasons _____

_____

_____

_____

continued on next page...

Were there any aspects of this guide that you particularly liked? ___________

____

____

Is there anything we could have done better? ___________

____

____

About you...

Name (*Mr/Mrs/Ms*) _______________________________

Address _______________________________

____

_______________________ Postcode _______________

Daytime tel nos _______________________________

Please only give us your mobile phone number if you wish to hear from us about other products and services from the AA and partners by text or mms.

Which age group are you in?

Under 25 ☐ 25–34 ☐ 35–44 ☐ 45–54 ☐ 55–64 ☐ 65+ ☐

How many trips do you make a year?

Less than one ☐ One ☐ Two ☐ Three or more ☐

Are you an AA member? Yes ☐ No ☐

About your trip...

When did you book? m m / y y When did you travel? m m / y y

How long did you stay? _______________________________

Was it for business or leisure? _______________________________

Did you buy any other travel guides for your trip?

If yes, which ones? _______________________________

Thank you for taking the time to complete this questionnaire. Please send it to us as soon as possible, and remember, you do not need a stamp (*unless posted outside the UK*).

Happy Holidays!

The information we hold about you will be used to provide the products and services requested and for identification, account administration, analysis, and fraud/loss prevention purposes. More details about how that information is used is in our privacy statement, which you'll find under the heading "Personal Information" in our terms and conditions and on our website: www.theAA.com. Copies are also available from us by post, by contacting the Data Protection Manager at AA, Southwood East, Apollo Rise, Farnborough, Hampshire GU14 OJW.

We may want to contact you about other products and services provided by us, or our partners (by mail, telephone) but please tick the box if you DO NOT wish to hear about such products and services from us by mail or telephone. ☐

The Atlas

Michelle Chaplow: *detail of the Palacios Nazaries*

www.theAA.com
The Automobile Association's website offers comprehensive and up-to-the-minute information covering AA-approved hotels, guest houses and B&Bs, restaurants and pubs in the UK; airport parking, insurance, European breakdown cover, European motoring advice, a ferry planner, European route planner, overseas fuel prices, a bookshop and much more.

www.aaa.com
AAA's website offers comprehensive information covering AAA-approved hotels and restaurants in the US. In addition, AAA can assist US citizens with obtaining a passport, reservations and tickets for cruise, tour, motorcoach, rail and air travel. AAA provides information on independent or escorted tours for individuals or groups and offers benefits on cruises, tours and travel packages.

The Foreign and Commonwealth Office
Country advice, traveller's tips, before you go information, checklists and more.
www.fco.gov.uk

Spanish National Tourist Office
www.tourspain.co.uk

GENERAL
UK Passport Service
www.ukpa.gov.uk

US passport information
www.travel.state.gov

Health Advice for Travellers
www.doh.gov.uk/traveladvice

BBC – Holiday
www.bbc.co.uk/holiday

The Full Universal Currency Converter
www.xe.com/ucc/full.shtml

Flying with Kids
www.flyingwithkids.com

Tourist atlas with photos, history, geography, art and tourist offices.
www.andalucia.org

Practical and background information. Accommodation, entertainment, real estate, living in Andalucia, consumer issues.
www.andalucia.com

Information on accommodation, restaurants, museums and major sites, fiestas. In Spanish only.
www.turismo.sevilla.org

Details of the Alhambra, other tourist attractions, hotels, where to eat, local transport.
www.granadatur.com

Information on the city, hotels, restaurants, museums, culture and the province of Cordoba. In Spanish only.
www.turiscordoba.es

Listings of rural accommodation.
www.raar.es

Information on the paradors throughout Spain.
www.parador.es

Accommodation, restaurants, beaches, golfing – all you need to know about the Costa del Sol.
www.visitcostadelsol.com

International website for the whole of Spain.
www.tourspain.es

TRAVEL
www.cheapflights.co.uk
www.thisistravel.co.uk
www.ba.com
www.worldairportguide.com

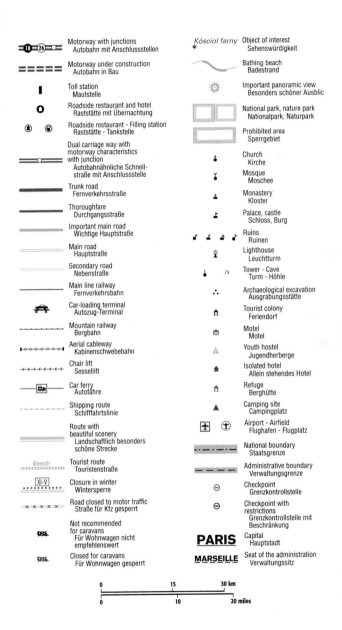

Motorway with junctions
Autobahn mit Anschlussstellen

Motorway under construction
Autobahn in Bau

Toll station
Mautstelle

Roadside restaurant and hotel
Raststätte mit Übernachtung

Roadside restaurant - Filling station
Raststätte - Tankstelle

Dual carriage way with
motorway characteristics
with junction
Autobahnähnliche Schnell-
straße mit Anschlussstelle

Trunk road
Fernverkehrsstraße

Thoroughfare
Durchgangsstraße

Important main road
Wichtige Hauptstraße

Main road
Hauptstraße

Secondary road
Nebenstraße

Main line railway
Fernverkehrsbahn

Car-loading terminal
Autozug-Terminal

Mountain railway
Bergbahn

Aerial cableway
Kabinenschwebebahn

Chair lift
Sessellift

Car ferry
Autofähre

Shipping route
Schifffahrtslinie

Route with
beautiful scenery
Landschaftlich besonders
schöne Strecke

Tourist route
Touristenstraße

Closure in winter
Wintersperre

Road closed to motor traffic
Straße für Kfz gesperrt

Not recommended
for caravans
Für Wohnwagen nicht
empfehlenswert

Closed for caravans
Für Wohnwagen gesperrt

Kósciol farny
Object of interest
Sehenswürdigkeit

Bathing beach
Badestrand

Important panoramic view
Besonders schöner Ausblic

National park, nature park
Nationalpark, Naturpark

Prohibited area
Sperrgebiet

Church
Kirche

Mosque
Moschee

Monastery
Kloster

Palace, castle
Schloss, Burg

Ruins
Ruinen

Lighthouse
Leuchtturm

Tower - Cave
Turm - Höhle

Archaeological excavation
Ausgrabungsstätte

Tourist colony
Feriendorf

Motel
Motel

Youth hostel
Jugendherberge

Isolated hotel
Allein stehendes Hotel

Refuge
Berghütte

Camping site
Campingplatz

Airport - Airfield
Flughafen - Flugplatz

National boundary
Staatsgrenze

Administrative boundary
Verwaltungsgrenze

Checkpoint
Grenzkontrollstelle

Checkpoint with
restrictions
Grenzkontrollstelle mit
Beschränkung

PARIS Capital
Hauptstadt

MARSEILLE Seat of the administration
Verwaltungssitz

0   15   30 km
0   10   20 miles

Maps © Mairs Geographischer Verlag / Falk Verlag, 73751 Ostfildern

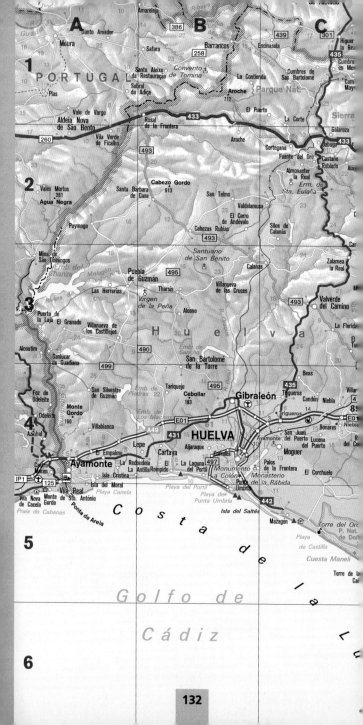

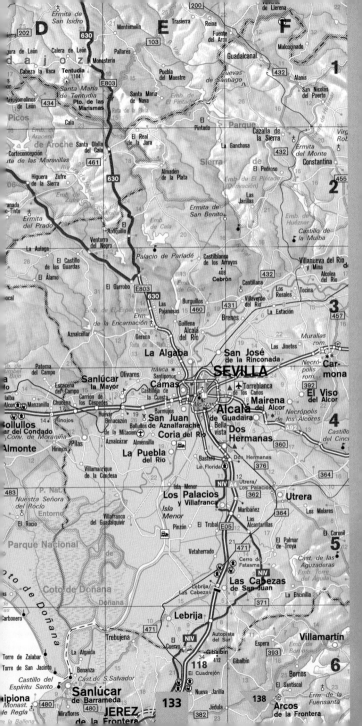

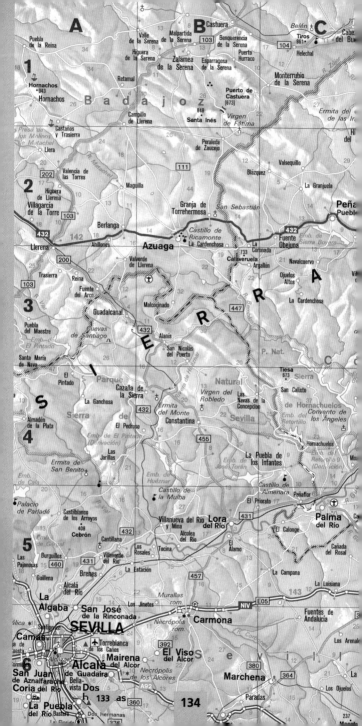

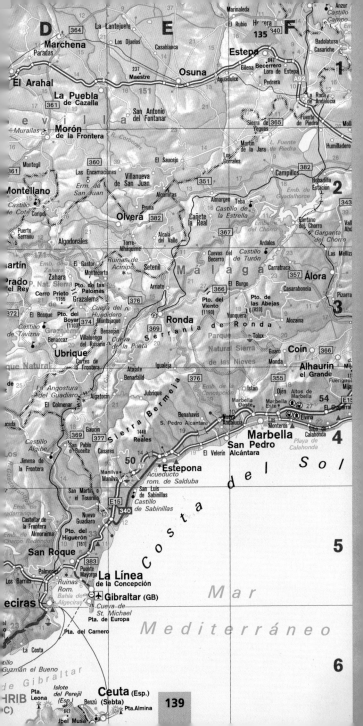

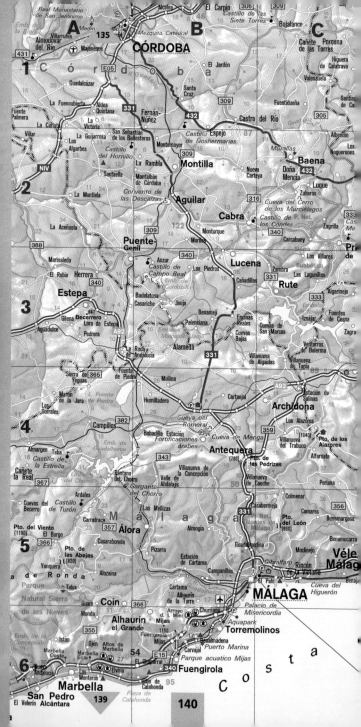

142

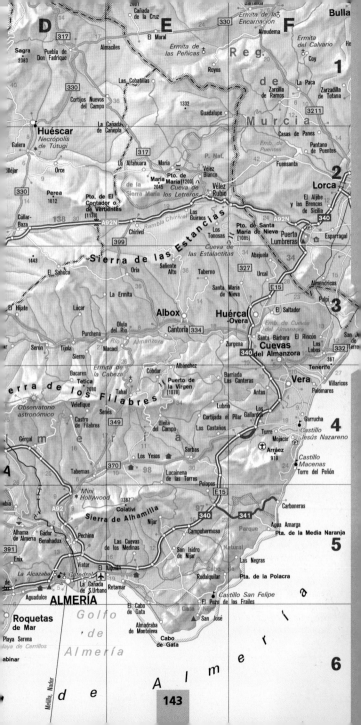

Sight Locator Index

This index relates to the atlas section on pages 132–143. We have given map references to the main sights of interest in the book. Some sights in the index may not be plotted on the atlas. Note: ibc – inside back cover

For the main index see pages 125–126